20 DAY TRIPS

20 DAY TRIPS

in and around the

Shawnee National Forest

**Larry P. and
Donna J. Mahan**

With a Foreword by Les Winkeler

Southern Illinois University Press
Carbondale and Edwardsville

16   15   14   13   4   3   2   1

All of the photographs in this book are by Larry P.
Mahan, with the exception of a select few taken by
Donna J. Mahan. The Mahans' dog, Gert, was an
enthusiastic participant and appears in some of the
images, usually in the company of Donna.

Library of Congress Cataloging-in-Publication Data
Mahan, Larry P., 1938–
20 day trips in and around the Shawnee National
Forest / Larry P. and Donna J. Mahan.
     p. cm.
Includes index.
ISBN 978-0-8093-3255-7 (pbk. : alk. paper) — ISBN
0-8093-3255-8 (pbk. : alk. paper) — ISBN 978-0-
8093-3256-4 (ebook) — ISBN 0-8093-3256-6 (ebook)
1. Shawnee National Forest Region (Ill.)—Guide-
books. 2. Shawnee National Forest (Ill.)—Guide-
books. I. Mahan, Donna, 1954– II. Title. III. Title:
Twenty day trips in and around the Shawnee
National Forest.
F547.S58M35 2013
977.3'992—dc23   2012033579

Contents

Special Attractions

QR (quick response) codes, like the one shown here, appear in the text for each day trip. With a barcode reader app on your smartphone or other portable electronic device, you can scan the QR codes in the text to find the starting point of each day trip on Google Maps. Then scroll to find the other points of interest.

If you have a GPS device, you can input the geographic coordinates given in the table in every day trip section.

Foreword

Les Winkeler

As the outdoors writer for the *Southern Illinoisan* I have spent most of the past 25 years extolling the beauty and diversity of Southern Illinois.

The southern tip of the state, nestled between the Mississippi and Ohio Rivers, is fundamentally different from the cornfields of central Illinois and the urban wonders of Chicago.

Larry and Donna Mahan have spent years exploring the hidden treasures of Southern Illinois. And, like anyone else who spends time in the region, they have learned to love and appreciate the scenic and biological diversity.

Read the book and allow the Mahans to direct you to the quiet beauty of Heron Pond, the spectacular scenery of Garden of the Gods, and the unspoiled grandeur of Piney Creek Ravine. Or discover history at Mound City National Cemetery and Fort Massac State Park, feel the wind as you bike on Tunnel Hill State Trail, and see reptiles migrate in spring and fall between the Pine Hills and LaRue Swamp. From Cave in Rock to Cairo, from Metropolis to Carbondale, there are dozens of ways to enjoyably spend your free time.

Read this book, follow the Mahans' advice, and you will discover a diversity that is sure to surprise you.

I'm betting decades of experience on it.

Preface

If you look at a map of Illinois, you will see at the southernmost tip the green-shaded section that represents the Shawnee National Forest. This is Illinois's only national forest, and on the map it looks like a very small segment of land compared to the rest of the state. Don't try to compare it to the rest of the state, though. It is a unique area, and its landmass of over 279,000 acres doesn't seem small at all when you are exploring it for yourself. If you are so inclined, you could spend two to three weeks hiking the entire River-to-River Trail, a distance of more than 160 miles, from the Ohio River to the Mississippi River. Or you could choose from a number of year-round recreational activities such as biking, bird watching, boating, camping, fishing, hiking, horseback riding, hunting, picnicking, rock climbing, wildlife viewing, and sampling the offerings of the numerous Southern Illinois wineries. You could take a scenic drive and view outstanding vistas, without leaving the comfort of your vehicle. You could take day hikes through places that are absolutely breathtaking. In the spring, many trails explode with color from masses of wildflowers, and the fall colors are equally brilliant and awe inspiring. Southern Illinois has many places of historical interest as well, from ancient Native American habitation areas to Civil War–era structures. So . . . where should you begin? Where are all these scenic areas, and how do you get there?

It has taken us several years, but we have come to know and appreciate many of the lovely natural places Southern Illinois has to offer, and we would like for you to get to know them, too. This series of day trips reflects a variety of different locales and activities. We have distilled and organized this information utilizing public domain information from the Internet, published materials from the Illinois Department of Natural Resources and the Shawnee National Forest, and our own experience. Travel distance and the efficient use of time were considered for each suggested trip. It has been a lengthy process devoted to photography, research, and organization of material to assemble this book. We hope that it will be a helpful resource for you and will encourage you to come and explore the many awesome places in southernmost Illinois.

Most of our day trips will require you to do some walking. As a general rule of thumb, these trips are designed for persons who are able-bodied and reasonably fit. The Shawnee National Forest is a wonderful place to explore on foot. Wheelchair accessibility is very limited, unfortunately, but will be noted where available.

Our attempt to provide the most accurate information possible has required, in many cases, numerous visits to our suggested locations as we tried to acquire just the right photograph or double check the clarity of our directions. We have hiked the trails and hunted and gathered the information that we hope will encourage you to take to a beautiful forest trail, walk the streets of a picturesque Southern Illinois town, or tour a historic building.

That said, we must conclude with this disclaimer: we assume no responsibility or liability for accidents or injuries that happen to those who use this book to explore the places described. We cannot predict or prevent actions by nature. In summer and winter, take into account the possibility of encountering extreme heat or cold, although the climate is relatively mild in Southern Illinois year-round. You will almost certainly encounter ticks, mosquitoes, or other insects in the summer, so be ready with insect repellant and appropriate clothing to make this a minor inconvenience. Each person must assume the risk of his or her own behavior and proceed with due caution. Be prepared. Stay on the trail. Respect private property and all the plant and animal life you encounter. Your soul will be refreshed and your spirit renewed.

Happy trails to you.

Acknowledgments

It has been a long process to bring this book to completion, and we would like to gratefully acknowledge the assistance we have received from the following people:

Jim and Mona Scantling, our friends from Elizabethtown, provided us with research assistance as well as bed and breakfast on numerous occasions when we were working in the eastern region of southernmost Illinois. Thanks, dear friends.

Jeremy Littrell, pilot of the *Shawnee Queen* River Taxi, filled us in on local history during our boat rides and gave us a personal tour of the Cave in Rock area.

John O'Dell, chairman of the River-to-River Trail Society, and Jim Ewers, president of the Shawnee Hills Wine Trail Association, graciously granted us interviews for this book.

Ed Cates took us hiking and shared his interest in Native American history and artifacts discovered in Southern Illinois. Thanks, Uncle Ed. That was really fun.

The "gang" at the Kozy Korner in Olive Branch listened with interest as we talked about the trails we hiked. Thanks also go to Ken Hill for showing us many interesting places in the western region of southernmost Illinois; Louise Ogg for giving us a special tour of the Custom House in Cairo and sharing local history; and John Watson for the tour of the Mound City National Cemetery and information about the Mound City Marine Ways. Special thanks go to Eleanor Duff for her steadfast enthusiasm for this project and her concern that we keep an eye out for snakes.

Barb Martin, our editor at SIU Press, enthusiastically supported this project from our first meeting and guided us through the publication process. Thanks, Barb. You helped to make this journey fun. Thanks also go to all of our friends and family members who encouraged us every step of the way during the many years it took us to complete this project!

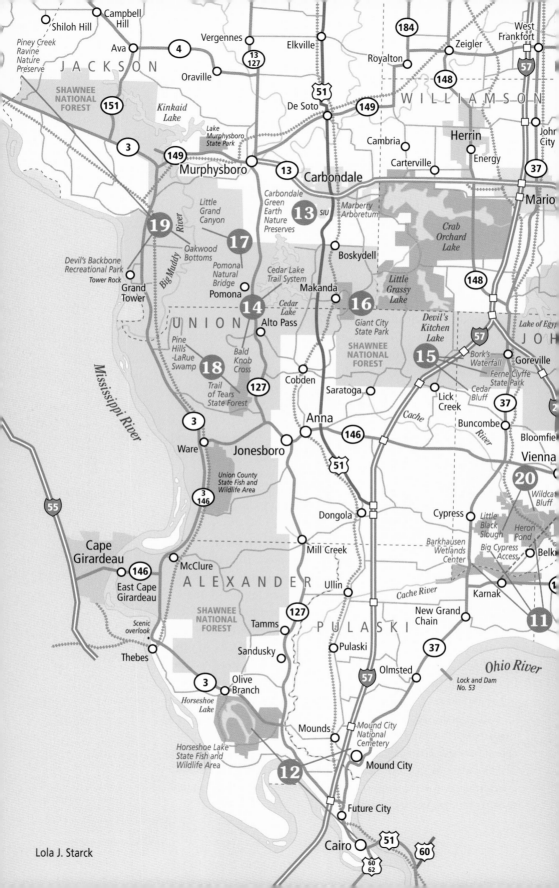

Lola J. Starck

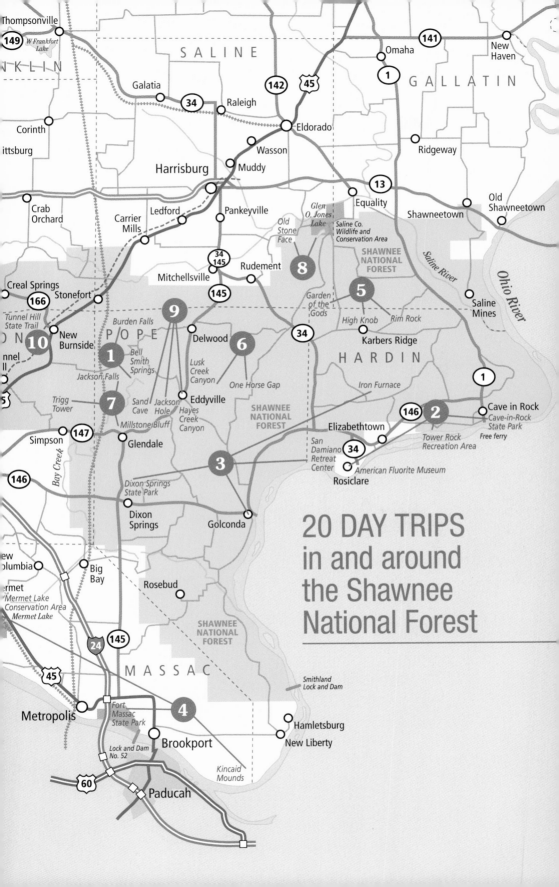

20 DAY TRIPS in and around the Shawnee National Forest

Shawnee National Forest Guidelines

Trail Difficulty Ratings

Easy: Little physical challenge. Trail is smooth, level, and wide.

Moderate: Requires a moderate degree of skill and is a reasonable physical challenge in steep terrain. Trail surface contains roots and rocks. You may come in contact with trees, limbs, and other vegetation. You may walk across streams.

Difficult: Requires a high degree of skill and is a difficult physical challenge in steep terrain. Trail is usually rough. You may come in contact with trees, limbs, and other vegetation. You may walk across streams.

Trail Etiquette

- Pack it in, pack it out
- Prevent erosion: avoid creating new trails and shortcuts; use switchbacks and stay on the existing trail
- Observe wildlife from a distance
- Minimize impact; stay in small groups
- Collect nothing from nature
- Be courteous of others; keep noise level down
- Keep pets on a leash
- Step off the trail when horses are passing
- Announce your presence to horseback riders
- Bury human waste and pack out toilet paper
- Pack out cigarette butts

Safety Tips

- Be prepared and notify someone of your plans; check the local weather forecast
- Carry a map, matches, compass, GPS unit, and cell phone (please note: a good majority of the Shawnee National Forest has little or no cell phone service)
- Bring extra water, food, and clothing
- Bring first-aid kit and flashlight
- Bring sunglasses, sunscreen, hand sanitizer, and water filter
- Avoid snakes and watch for poison ivy
- Avoid hiking during fall and spring gun hunting seasons
- Wear insect repellant
- Review emergency phone numbers for the area(s) in which you plan to travel and rely on them or 911 in the event of an emergency

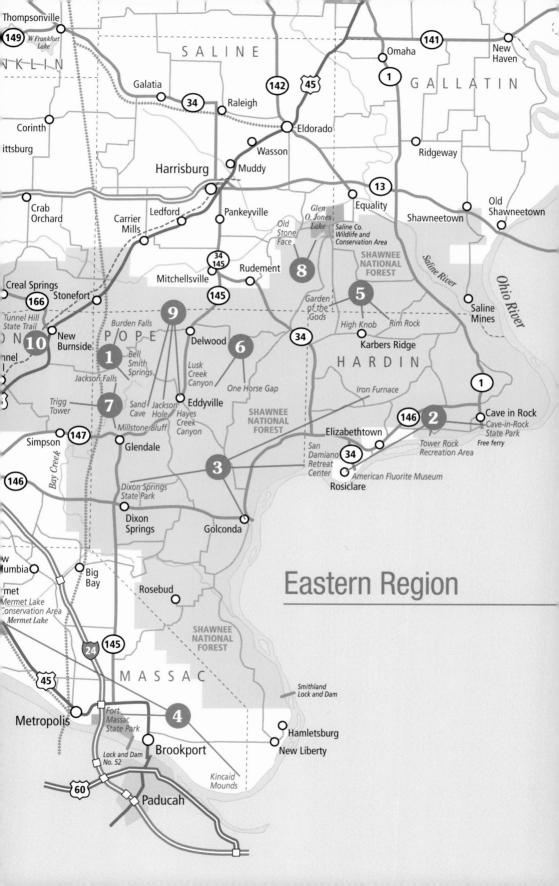

Eastern Region

> *The human spirit needs places where nature has not been rearranged by the hand of man.*
> *—Author unknown*

Day Trip 1

Mill Branch Trail, Bell Smith Springs

When we started hiking in Southern Illinois, **Burden Falls** was one of the first places we visited. Both Burden Falls and Bell Smith Springs are prime examples of the trademark land features of the Shawnee National Forest—sandstone cliffs and high bluffs intermingled with heavily forested areas. Throw in a spectacular waterfall, as found at Burden Falls, and you have a place of irresistible appeal.

For this day trip, you will need a good pair of hiking shoes and a certain amount of physical agility to negotiate the trail. Cross the stone glade and locate the rim trail on the opposite side of the canyon from the parking lot. In the wet season, you may have to cross water from the upper falls area to reach this

- Burden Falls
- Bell Smith Springs

3

side of the canyon. The depth of the water can vary depending upon rainfall; be aware that flowing water is treacherous to cross. Always be mindful of safety and proceed with caution. Heavy precipitation does provide the optimum viewing experience for Burden Falls, however, so if you are here after a big rain, you will be rewarded with a wonderful view. Even in the dry part of summer, the area is well worth a visit to hike along its sandstone ledges and into the rock-lined canyon that provides the backdrop for the beautiful waterfall.

The upper trail comes to a dead end after a short distance, at which point you will be on top of the falls and can look down on the canyon below. To view the falls from the canyon floor, find the crawl space under a raised boulder and descend to the bottom of the falls. This is the shortest way to the canyon floor, but you must be rather nimble. Or, you can stay on the parking lot side of the canyon and take the longer trail that will eventually bring you to the canyon floor. The walking is easier along this narrow but well-defined forest trail. From the canyon floor, you will have an upward view of the waterfall. You will still have to scramble back up the rocks to complete your route to the parking lot unless you retrace your hike through the forest. The lower falls is the highest and most impressive, but in

Burden Falls

its entirety, Burden Falls is a series of cascades and sandstone cataracts totaling among the tallest in Illinois.

Next, drive over to beautiful **Bell Smith Springs**, an area with eight miles of interconnected trails divided into four labeled trails of varying distance and scenic highlights. Each of the trails is marked with a different color diamond periodically placed upon trees along the route. Read the interpretive sign at the main parking lot trailhead explaining the unique ecosystem and history of the Bell Smith Springs area. Choose a trail based on your time schedule and interests.

The surface of the trails is dirt and rock, making the going difficult at times. The canyon floor from the Natural Bridge Trail, for instance, is reached via the descent of a stone stairway, accessible only by the able-bodied. The Mill Branch Trail, one of our favorites, features a spectacular stream-carved gorge. In addition to the high sandstone cliffs and rock features favored by hikers, there is a diverse variety of habitats for plants and bird species, making this a multiuse area for nature lovers and a favorite destination within the Shawnee National Forest.

It is a good idea to obtain trail maps and brochures from the Forest Service before hiking any given area. This free information is a great aid when visiting a new place. Bell Smith Springs is a large area to explore. You may choose one or two trails and hike for an hour or two, or you could spend one or two days hiking the entire area. Spring is an especially wonderful time to visit, when the forest floor comes alive with colorful wildflowers.

Just so you know . . .

- The 3,775-acre parcel of land designated the **Burden Falls Wilderness Area** contains a second-growth oak/ hickory forest in addition to the upper and lower waterfalls areas.

- **Bell Smith Springs'** wooded slopes are dominated by wonderful old oak and hickory trees, while the bottom of the canyon features huge beech and tulip trees.

- Bird watchers have been known to spot tanagers, sparrows, pileated woodpeckers, eastern phoebes, and several different species of vireos.

- The **Natural Bridge Trail** at Bell Smith Springs features the highest natural bridge in the Shawnee National Forest, with a 125-foot span and a 30-foot arch.

- Bell Smith Springs provides habitats for over 700 species of flowering plants, ferns, and lichens, making it home to about 20 percent of the total number of plants and lichens in the state.

- The **Red Bud Campground** at Bell Smith Springs is open March 15–December 15. It is a primitive campground with 21 heavily wooded, secluded sites. Drinking water and detailed maps of the Bell Smith Springs Trail System are available. For information, contact the Hidden Springs Ranger District at Vienna, 618-658-2111.

Natural Bridge Trail, Bell Smith Springs

Rock stairs, Bell Smith Springs

Day Trip	Landforms and Features	Distance (round-trip) and Duration	Difficulty	Facilities
Burden Falls 37°33′48.49″ N 88°38′32.62″ W	Waterfalls and steep canyon	100 yards–1 mile, 30 minutes–2 hours	Moderate–difficult	Parking area
Bell Smith Springs Interpretive site 37°31′8.25″ N 88°39′25.40″ W	Sandstone cliffs, deep canyons	**4 labeled trails** **General area** (white diamond)— 1.5 miles, 1 hour **Natural Bridge** (yellow diamond)— 1.5 miles, 1 hour **Mill Branch** (red diamond)— 2 miles, 2 hours **Sentry Bluff** (blue diamond)— 3.2 miles, 3 hours	Moderate–difficult	Ample parking, restrooms, water, picnic tables, camping sites, interpretive signs

Upper level, Little Burden Falls

Directions

To reach **Burden Falls** from Marion, travel east on IL-13 for 22 miles to Harrisburg. Turn right (south) on IL-145 and go 11 miles to Delwood. Turn right (west) on Burden Falls Road (Forest Road 402), which is a gravel road, and continue for 4.5 miles to Burden Falls parking lot.

From Burden Falls to **Bell Smith Springs**, continue west on Burden Falls Road for .5 mile to Forest Road 447. Turn left (south) and proceed 2 miles to Forest Road 848 (Bell Smith Springs entrance), then turn right (southwest), which leads to the Bell Smith Springs main parking area.

Day Trip 2

View of Cave-in-Rock from the Ohio River

Cave-in-Rock State Park consists of 204 acres of land, including wooded areas, rugged bluffs along the Ohio River, and the 55-foot-wide cave carved out of limestone rock. The famous cave is so steeped in folklore and legend that it is difficult to be certain of its true history. It is known that in 1797, Samuel Mason, an evil proprietor to be sure, converted the cavern into a tavern and subjected unwary patrons to thievery and murder. Colorful stories abound about other notorious characters said to have a connection to the cave. Whatever its history, this distinctive landmark has drawn visitors for hundreds of years. The lure of that wide-open mouth cannot be denied.

- Cave-in-Rock State Park
- Tower Rock
- Elizabethtown
- Rosiclare

View of Ohio River from inside Cave-in-Rock

Once inside the park, the actual cave is easy to find with posted signs and a well-trodden path that follows the Ohio River shoreline. The cave is not wheelchair accessible, and there are stairs to climb at one point, but the hike is short and of moderate difficulty. Do not miss the view from any of the beautiful picnic sites atop the bluffs overlooking the river, accessible by driving the one-way mile loop in the park. Each site provides a little different perspective of the river, and all are outstanding vistas.

After spending time at the park, drive the short distance over to **Tower Rock**, the highest point along the Ohio River on the Illinois shore. The hike from the parking area is short but a bit steep. The trailhead is marked with a sign, and the trail is well worn by many visitors over the years. From the top of this bluff, there are several vantage points that offer a dazzling view of the Ohio River. The trail brings you right along the edge of the bluff, so watch your step.

From here, travel to **Elizabethtown**, a picturesque little village of about 350 people situated on the Ohio River. The oldest continuously operating Baptist church in Illinois, the First Baptist Church of Elizabethtown, can be found here. Established in

Tower Rock bluff

1806, the church, originally known as Big Creek Baptist Church, has served its congregation for more than 200 years and counting. The congregation has been at its present location since 1877, when the current building was dedicated. Another historic structure not to be missed is the Rose Hotel, founded in 1812 as McFarland's Tavern and operating as a bed and breakfast at the present time. This landmark structure, overlooking the Ohio River, is owned by the state of Illinois and includes a gazebo on the well-manicured grounds as well as a gift shop that is open to the public.

Complete your day with a visit to the historic village of **Rosiclare.** In 1843, the discovery of lead and fluorspar began Rosiclare's growth into the largest fluorspar mining operation in the nation at that time. Today, the American Fluorite Museum, in the former office building of the Rosiclare Lead and Fluorspar Mining Company near downtown Rosiclare, is open seasonally from May through October, Thursday through Sunday, 1:00– 4:00 P.M., and Saturday, 10:00 A.M.–4:00 P.M. There is a small admission fee to tour the museum.

Just so you know . . .

- The campground within **Cave-in-Rock State Park,** 1 New State Park Road, provides electricity, showers, restrooms, and dumping stations on nicely wooded sites. Call 618-289-4325 for information.

- The **Cave-in-Rock State Park Restaurant and Lodge,** within the park, features family-style food and rents nearby cabins with private patio decks overlooking the Ohio River. For information, call 618-289-4545 or visit www.caveinrockkaylors.com.

- The **First Baptist Church** at **Elizabethtown** is at Market and Locust Streets. For information, call 618-287-2861.

- The **Rose Hotel** in Elizabethtown is at 92 Main Street. There are five guest rooms, some with balconies overlooking the Ohio River. Call 618-287-2872 for information.

- The **River Rose Inn,** 1 Main Street, is another bed and breakfast in Elizabethtown. It also has views of the Ohio River. Call 618-287-8811 for information.

- The **American Fluorite Museum** is on Main Street, PO Box 755, Rosiclare, IL, 62982. Call 618-285-3513 for information.

- The **Rosiclare City Park** offers a wheelchair accessible River Walk with benches for those who want to relax. The park provides shelters, picnic tables, playground equipment, and a fenced-in playground.

- **Rosiclare River View Campsites,** in the city park, are equipped with electricity, water, and boat docking facilities. Call Rosiclare City Hall at 618-285-3445 for information.

Rose Hotel, Elizabethtown

Day Trip	Landforms and Features	Distance (round-trip) and Duration	Difficulty	Facilities
Cave-In-Rock State Park Cave Parking 37°28′06.1″ N 88°09′34.6″ W	Rugged bluffs, famous cave, scenic vistas of Ohio River	1-mile loop drive through park .25-mile hike to cave and view river from bluff, 2 hours	Easy– Moderate	Restrooms, water, cabins, gift shop/restaurant, wheelchair accessible picnic sites, campground
Tower Rock 37°27′27.23″ N 88°13′43.76″ W	160-foot bluff overlooking Ohio River	300 yards, .75 hour	Moderate	Picnic tables, parking area
Elizabethtown Rose Hotel 37°26′42.4″ N 88°18′17.0″ W	Ohio River town	1–2 hours to explore the town	Easy	Food, water, restrooms, gift shop, bed and breakfast lodging, wheelchair accessible
Rosiclare American Fluorite Museum 37°25′23.8″ N 88°20′50.2″ W	Ohio River town	1 hour to explore the town	Easy	Food, water, restrooms, museum, gift shop, wheelchair accessible

American Fluorite Museum, Rosiclare

Directions

From Harrisburg to **Cave-in-Rock State Park**, go east on IL-13 (Poplar Street) for approximately 14 miles to IL-1. Turn right (south) on IL-1 and go 21 miles to Cave in Rock. Follow directional signs for .5 mile to the park entrance. At the camping sign, keep right for the 1-mile driving loop, which includes the lodge, cabins, and bluff vistas. Cave parking is well marked.

To reach **Tower Rock** from downtown Cave in Rock, take W. Clay Street (Tower Rock sign) left (west) for 4.2 miles to Tower Rock entrance sign. Turn left (south), keeping left as the road winds, and continue for .8 mile to parking lot.

From Tower Rock to **Elizabethtown**, retrace route to entrance, turn left (west) on Tower Rock Road, and continue for 3 miles to IL-146. Turn left (southwest), continuing for 3 miles to downtown Elizabethtown.

From Elizabethtown to **Rosiclare**, take IL-146 west for 2.5 miles, turning left (south) on IL-34 at Rosiclare sign. Continue for 2.4 miles to entrance of American Fluorite Museum on your right.

The true meaning of life is to plant trees, under whose shade you do not expect to sit.
—Nelson Henderson

Day Trip 3

Iron Furnace

When you drive through the gates at **Dixon Springs State Park**, you will immediately sense the ancient feel of the place. It is quiet and serene now, but you can still catch a whisper of the past inhabitants as you gaze upon the mature trees and realize that many of them have been standing here for over 100 years. Various tribes of Native Americans, such as the Algonquins, are said to have used Dixon Springs as a favorite camping ground, but by the early 1830s, most of them were gone. Settlers began populating the area, and a community developed around the seven natural springs. The landscape is beautiful, with a brook flowing through the valley framed by bold cliffs and a variety of forest trees, including oak, pine, sycamore, and hickory. For a

- Dixon Springs State Park
- Golconda
- Iron Furnace
- San Damiano Retreat Center

time, this idyllic spot buzzed with activity as a 19th-century health spa. The mineral-enriched water of the springs lured guests from Kentucky and Indiana in addition to those from Illinois. One remaining "health" spring is still active, but now people come to enjoy the shaded picnic areas and hike the trails, perhaps thinking of the time when Native Americans walked the same route.

In 1798, ten miles away, Major James Lusk began a ferry business on the Illinois side of the Ohio River, the success of which helped establish the town of **Golconda**. Lusk died early in the project, and his wife, Sarah, carried on, becoming the first woman to receive a ferry license from the governor of the Indiana Territory, William Henry Harrison. Golconda was first named Sarahsville and thrived during the heyday of river traffic. Now it is a small, quiet village with about 760 residents. Many of the old brick buildings downtown date from the middle to the later 1800s, and a number of homes from that era survive in private hands today. The historic Buel House, however, is owned by the Illinois Historic Preservation Agency, as is the Davidson Cabin that sits next to it. The Buel House, built about 1840, is not the oldest house in town but is believed to be the oldest continuously occupied by the builder's family, having only two other

Ghost Dance Trail, Dixon Springs

View of the Ohio River from San Damiano Retreat Center

owners after the last family member died in 1986 at the age of 97. The second of the non-family owners presented it to the Illinois Historic Preservation Agency in 1992, and it is now open to the public. Hours of operation vary, as many of these attractions are dependent on volunteer labor.

Continue your day at the Illinois **Iron Furnace**. Active from 1839 to 1883, it was the first charcoal-fired furnace in Illinois. At one time, 100 or more families were living in the area, and a post office named Illinois Furnace was opened on November 2, 1846. Some of the pig iron smelted there prior to 1861 was utilized at the Mound City Marine Ways for building ironclad gunboats used in the Civil War. Today, the reconstructed furnace can be viewed at its original location. None of the community buildings remain. If you stand in this quiet spot and look at the massive iron furnace, it will be easy for you to imagine the bustling activity that defined this place in a bygone era.

A visit to the **San Damiano Retreat Center**, a 200-acre site atop a cliff above the Ohio River, is a relaxing way to finish the day. Overnight guests have a view of Kentucky on the opposite shore as they unwind on their private deck overlooking the river. Stop at the hacienda-style visitor center and receive information in the gift shop about touring the grounds. In addition to the stunning views of the river, there are quiet walkways through the woods and a remarkable 35-foot bronze statue of the Good Shepherd. A trailhead near the cabins leads from the top of the bluff down to the Ohio shoreline. Whether or not you spend a night here, bask in the aura of peacefulness that emanates from this memorable place.

Just so you know . . .

- **Dixon Springs State Park**, RR 2, Box 178, IL-146, Golconda, IL, 62938, is open year-round except Christmas Day and New Year's Day. For information, call 618-949-3394.

- A nice, privately owned swimming pool, with bathhouse and 45-foot water slide, is within easy walking distance of the Dixon Springs campground. In season, campers may use the swimming pool and shower facilities for a reasonable fee during regular hours of operation.

- At the former village site within the park boundary, the old church buildings still remain.

- **The Chocolate Factory**, on IL-146 across from the entrance to Dixon Springs State Park, offers a wide variety of chocolate treats and ice cream for sale. Year-round business hours are Monday–Saturday, 9:00 A.M.–5:00 P.M. Call 618-949-3829 or visit www.thechocolatefactory.net.

- The **Buel House**, 328 South Columbus Avenue near downtown Golconda, is designated as a Historical Point of Interest on the National Historic Trail of Tears. In the spring and summer of 1838, more than 15,000 Cherokee Indians were removed by the US Army from their homelands in North Carolina, Georgia, Tennessee, and

Buel House and Davidson Cabin, Golconda

Alabama and forced to travel over 1,000 miles to Indian Territory, which is now Oklahoma. The Trail of Tears route across Southern Illinois from Golconda to the Mississippi River was less than 60 miles, but a harsh winter took a tremendous toll, accounting for the highest mortality rate of any state the Cherokees passed through. In Pope County, all of the detachments crossed the Ohio River by way of Berry's Ferry from Kentucky, landing at the mouth of Lusk Creek. From there, the detachments traveled through Golconda.

- For information about **Golconda** attractions, call 618-683-6246 or visit www.visitgolconda.com.

- The **San Damiano Retreat Center** has conference facilities as well as deluxe cabins and suites for rent. For information, call 618-285-3507 or visit www.sandamianoretreat.com.

Day Trip	Landforms and Features	Distance (round-trip) and Duration	Difficulty	Facilities
Dixon Springs State Park Entrance 37°22′49.1″ N 88°39′57.7″ W	801-acre park, sandstone formations, boulders, springs	Ghost Dance Trail and area springs— 1.75 miles, 2 hours	Moderate	Outdoor privies, water, picnic and playground areas, campground with electricity and water
Golconda Buel House 37°21′51.9″ N 88°29′04.3″ W	Ohio River town	2.5 hours to explore the town	Easy	Food, water, restrooms, gift and antique shops
Iron Furnace 37°29′55.98″ N 88°19′39.53″ W	Valley, low hills	Big Creek Trail— .75 mile, 1 hour	Easy	Picnic shelter, parking area
San Damiano Retreat Center Visitor center parking lot 37°25′34.2″ N 88°24′55.5″ W	Huge bluff overlooking Ohio River, walking trails, 35-foot bronze statue of the Good Shepherd	400-yard walk along bluff, 30 minutes	Easy	Cabins, restrooms, gift shop at visitor center

Directions

From Vienna, go east on IL-146 for 13.2 miles to **Dixon Springs State Park**. A large sign marks the entrance to the park on your left.

From Dixon Springs, continue east on IL-146 for 10.1 miles to downtown **Golconda**.

From Golconda, continue north on IL-146 for 13.1 miles. Turn left (north) on Iron Furnace Road and continue 3.8 miles to **Iron Furnace**.

From Iron Furnace, retrace route to IL-146 and turn right (west) on IL-146 for 4 miles. Look for the **San Damiano** sign at the junction of IL-34 and IL-146. As the sign indicates, turn left (south) and continue for 2.5 miles to San Damiano entrance sign. Turn left (south) at the entrance sign and continue .3 mile to the visitor center. Turn right into the parking area.

Those who contemplate the beauty of the earth find
reserves of strength that will endure as long as life lasts.
—Rachel Carson

Day Trip 4

Fort Massac State Park

Fort Massac State Park, dedicated in 1908, is Illinois's first state park. Overlooking the Ohio River, the park's historical roots go all the way back to 1757, when the French erected the first fort on the site. The British took it over in 1765, and the Chickasaw Indians burned it down after the French and Indian War. It was rebuilt after the Revolutionary War but destroyed again by the New Madrid earthquake of 1811–12. The fort was next rebuilt as a fortification during the War of 1812 and served briefly as a training camp during the Civil War, which was the last time US troops were stationed at the site. Reconstructed in the early 1970s to resemble the American fort, the site draws over 100,000 visitors each year. The park consists of 1,470 acres and

- Fort Massac State Park

- Kincaid Mounds

- Mermet Lake Conservation Area

offers hiking trails, fishing, picnicking, and camping throughout the year. This is a great place to bring the family for a day trip or a weekend camping trip.

The city of Metropolis, where the park is located, also boasts the unique attraction of being the "home" of Superman, hero of comic books, movies, and television. The Superman Museum is downtown near the huge statue on the square, where you will find everything you ever wanted to know and more about Superman in all his incarnations.

An interesting side trip from Metropolis is a visit to the **Kincaid Mounds**. This 105-acre archaeological site features 11 Mississippian era Indian mounds, dating A.D. 900–1400. The site is managed by the Illinois Historic Preservation Agency and owned by the state. The 30-foot tall mounds are in a plaza area, which formed a community and social center; they can be seen from a viewing platform that contains interpretive signs to aid in visualizing the ancient community. Walking on the mounds is not permitted.

Kincaid Mounds

Winter guests at Mermet Lake Conservation Area

Another interesting side trip from Metropolis is the **Mermet Lake Conservation Area**. Primarily developed for duck hunting, the water in the 450-acre shallow lake is dropped two feet each fall to accommodate duck hunters. After waterfowl season, the water is returned to pool stage. At the southeast corner of Mermet Lake Conservation Area, 43 acres have been set aside for rare and endangered species. Hunting for doves, deer, squirrels, rabbits, and quail is permitted in designated areas. In addition, Mermet Lake has two hiking trails, found at the west end of the preserve in an old-growth forest that includes pin oak, sweet gum, and swamp white oak. The Flatwoods Loop Trail includes tree identification markers and conveniently spaced benches. The Bluebird Hiking Trail features prairie grass and native plants and flowers in an open meadow setting. Bird watching is another favorite activity at Mermet Lake.

Just so you know . . .

- **Fort Massac State Park** has a full-facility campground, boat ramps, and picnic areas in addition to a museum and reconstructed fort. A popular attraction is the **Fort Massac Encampment**, held every year on the third weekend in October. This event offers military drills, mock battles, food, crafts, and music provided by civilian and military reenactors portraying life as it was lived over 200 years ago. For more information about the encampment, call 618-524-4712. For more info about the park's activities, call 618-524-9321 or visit the Illinois Department of Natural Resources at http://www.dnr.illinois.gov.

- Also in the area, the **Massac Forest Nature Preserve** includes 244 acres, featuring a wide variety of trees, wildflowers, and birds.

- **Harrah's Metropolis Casino & Hotel** complex, featuring the *North Star* riverboat, where the gambling action is located, has become the biggest tourist draw in the area. The complex includes a 258-room hotel, a multipurpose event center, a restaurant, banquet facilities, and a gift shop.

Superman statue, Metropolis

- Metropolis holds an annual **Superman Celebration** the second week in June. The event includes carnival rides, crafts, and food concessions. For more information, call the Metro-Chamber at 800-949-5740.

- Southern Illinois University Carbondale provides an eight-week field school that has taken place at **Kincaid Mounds** every summer for the past several years. The school continues to discover new artifacts from the site and hopes to understand how the site developed and why it declined and was abandoned.

- **Mermet Lake Conservation Area** has served as a site for the Archery Shooters Association (ASA) Pro/Am shooting competition for many years. This family-oriented event features archers trying to qualify for the world championship. The Mermet shoot is one of six ASA championship meets. For more information on Mermet Lake, call the Illinois Department of Natural Resources office at Belknap at 618-524-5577.

Day Trip	Landforms and Features	Distance (round-trip) and Duration	Difficulty	Facilities
Fort Massac State Park Entrance 37°08′41.0″ N 88°42′54.7″ W	1,470-acre lowlands near Ohio River	200 yards–1 mile, 2–3 hours to walk site and explore fort	Easy	Wheelchair accessible museum and gift shop, food, water, picnic areas, restrooms, ample parking, campground
Kincaid Mounds Parking area 37°04′47.2″ N 88°29′25.4″ W	105-acre bottomlands with 30-foot-tall mounds	View mounds from platform, 30 minutes	Easy	Parking area, wheelchair accessible viewing platform with picnic table
Mermet Lake Conservation Area Entrance 37°16′28.1″ N 88°50′53.3″ W	450-acre floodplain lake	Flatwood Trail— 1 mile, 1–2 hours Bluebird Trail— 1 mile, 1–2 hours	Easy Easy	Restrooms, water, picnic area, fishing, hiking, boating (rentals available), hunting in designated areas

George R. Clark statue, Fort Massac State Park

Directions

From Harrisburg to Metropolis, take IL-45 south for 27.1 miles to I-24, just north of Vienna. Merge onto I-24, and go south for 23.2 miles to exit 37. Turn right (west) on IL-45, go 3 miles, and enter **Fort Massac State Park** at 1308 E. 5th Street.

To reach **Kincaid Mounds** from Fort Massac State Park entrance, take IL-45 east for 7 miles, turning left (east) on Unionville Road. Go 6.25 miles east to New Cut Road, turn right (south), and go 3.5 miles to New Liberty Road. Turn left (east) and go .5 mile to the mounds parking area.

To reach **Mermet Lake Conservation Area** from Metropolis, take IL-45 north for 11 miles to Mermet Lake Conservation Area entrance (on your left).

Day Trip 5

Camel Rock, Garden of the Gods

If there is one well-known spot within the Shawnee National Forest, it is the **Garden of the Gods**. And within the Garden of the Gods, unquestionably the best known of the many fabulous sandstone rock formations is Camel Rock. In fact, Camel Rock was chosen to represent the state of Illinois in the US Mint's "America the Beautiful quarters program. Beginning in 2010, the commemorative quarters will feature the familiar 1923 portrait of George Washington on one side and a national park or other national site for each state on the reverse. The quarters will be issued sequentially each year, in the order in which the featured site was first established as a national park or site. The Illinois coin featuring Camel Rock will not be available until 2016.

- Garden of the Gods
- High Knob
- Rim Rock

Observation Trail, Garden of the Gods

But don't wait until 2016 to view the famous Camel Rock on the back of a quarter. Come see it in person, any time of the year, and you won't be disappointed. There are large and well-maintained parking areas and clearly marked trails. Choose one and you will hike through oak and hickory woodlands deep in the heart of the Shawnee National Forest or past ancient sandstone boulders named after the familiar images they resemble, such as Noah's Ark, Camel Rock, Anvil Rock, Table Rock, Devil's Smoke Stack, and Chimney Rock. Signage indicates that this area of the Shawnee Hills is part of an ancient mountain range around 320 million years old. Incredible! Even if it isn't that old, the natural elements and processes of wind, rain, freezing, and thawing have obviously been at work here for a very long time.

Stunning views can also be had from **High Knob**, a 930-foot sandstone hill overlooking panoramic forest vistas to the south, west, and east. The drive to the summit of High Knob is a bit of a challenge. Each time we have been there, the rock and dirt road has had deep ruts and washed-out sections requiring slow and careful driving. Once on top, there is a small parking area, a privy, a couple of picnic tables, and the beautiful vista.

Keep in mind that High Knob and Garden of the Gods are both wilderness areas. Trails around the High Knob rim are rugged and difficult. Hikers must use extreme caution as a fall from any of the high cliffs would almost certainly cause death or serious injury. Appreciate the beauty but respect the terrain.

From High Knob, drive over to **Rim Rock** and hike the National Trail. You may choose between the upper and lower portions of the trail. The upper trail is paved and less strenuous for hikers. You will see sheer cliffs and massive sandstone boulders as you walk through a hardwood forest and a red cedar grove, past remnants of a stone wall built by prehistoric Native Americans, and to an observation platform. From here we recommend descending the wooden staircase and stone steps to the lower trail (dirt surface) that leads along the base of the bluff, past the Ox-lot Cave, and finally back to the parking lot.

Each of these areas is awesome in any season. Without seasonal foliage, the rock formations are most visible in winter. Snow- and ice-covered cliffs can provide breathtaking photo opportunities for those with an adventurous spirit.

National Trail, Rim Rock

Just so you know . . .

- There is no admission fee for **Garden of the Gods**, and it is open all year. Pets are allowed on a leash. The main parking area has toilets nearby and is the entry point for the Observation Trail, the popular half-mile hike that features the famous Camel Rock. There are many miles of marked hiking trails. Maps and other information are available from the Shawnee National Forest district office in Harrisburg; call 618-253-7114.

- **Pharaoh Campground** at Garden of the Gods has 12 primitive campsites. Call Hidden Springs Ranger District in Vienna for information at 618-658-2111.

- Shady picnic sites with beautiful cliff vistas are scattered throughout the Garden of the Gods.

- Garden of the Gods is a very popular spot, especially on weekends. Go throughout the week to encounter fewer people.

- **Rim Rock** is only a short distance from **Pounds Hollow Lake**. Beaver Trail connects the Rim Rock valley floor to Pounds Hollow less than two miles away. Signs along the trail indicate a trailhead intersection where you can hike to the lake, or follow the bluff to the right and continue back to the Rim Rock parking area.

Garden of the Gods vista

Day Trip	Landforms and Features	Distance (round-trip) and Duration	Difficulty	Facilities
Garden of the Gods Observation site 37°36′14.23″ N 88°23′7.41″ W	Sandstone escarpments, giant boulders	Observation Trail—.5 mile, 1 hour Total trail system—5.5 miles, 4 hours	Easy–difficult	Toilets, water, picnic tables, ample parking area, primitive camping
High Knob 37°36′0.01″ N 88°19′41.70″ W	930-foot sandstone hill	Hike around the rim area—200 yards–1 mile, 1 hour	Easy–difficult	Toilet, picnic tables, limited parking
Rim Rock Picnic area 37°36′8.76″ N 88°16′41.97″ W	Sheer cliffs, massive boulders, shelter cave	National Trail—1.5 miles, 1.5–2 hours	Moderate–difficult	Toilets, picnic tables, ample parking, interpretive signs

High Knob vista

Directions

To reach **Garden of the Gods** from Harrisburg, go south on IL-34/145 for 7 miles. Turn left (southeast) on IL-34 and continue for another 7.5 miles to Herod. Continue 2 miles, turning left (east) on Karbers Ridge Road (County Road 1500 E). Travel east for 3 miles to the Garden of the Gods sign, turning left (north) and continuing 2 miles to the park entrance. Follow posted signs for 1 mile to main parking area.

To reach **High Knob** from Garden of the Gods, retrace route (south) to Karbers Ridge Road. Turn left (east), traveling 1.5 miles to the village of Karbers Ridge. Turn left (north) at High Knob posted sign (Forest Road 33). Go approximately 2 miles and turn right (east) at a horse camp. Drive past the horse camp, uphill, for .5 mile to the summit of High Knob. Road may be rough and rutted.

To reach **Rim Rock** from High Knob, retrace route to the village of Karbers Ridge. Turn left (east) on Karbers Ridge Road, going 3.8 miles to the Rim Rock entrance sign. Turn left (north), continuing a few hundred yards to the parking lot. A large trail map is posted for information.

*In wilderness I sense the miracle of life, and behind
it our scientific accomplishments fade to trivia.
—Charles A. Lindbergh*

Day Trip 6

Indian Kitchen at Lusk Creek Wilderness Area

Eat a hearty breakfast and strap on your very best hiking shoes
for this day trip through two uniquely beautiful but challenging areas. You will find the scenery breathtaking, and not
just from energy expenditure, as you hike through some of the
loveliest forest areas that we have seen.

Start with the Indian Kitchen Trail in the **Lusk Creek Canyon
Wilderness Area**. You will really get that "walking through the
wilderness" feeling as you head deeper and deeper into the forest
on a single-file dirt track. The sense of a bygone time and place

- Lusk Creek Canyon
  Wilderness Area

- One Horse Gap

is strong in this area. The stillness of the forest will envelop you as you pass through stand after stand of stately pines. The path is clear and follows a mostly level terrain. This is not a place to stray off the trail, though; it would be easy to become disoriented wandering through this dense forest. Signs are posted along the trail, encouraging you to continue toward Indian Kitchen. When you reach a large clearing with a hitching area for horseback riders, you will have come to the last segment of your hike. From here, there is a marked contrast in the terrain. Now you will be making a sharp descent, approximately a quarter of a mile, over rocky terrain into the Lusk Creek Canyon area. You will see a huge sandstone bluff rising in front of your eyes, dwarfing the creek that runs through the valley floor. Take a moment to sit and gaze at this wall of stone before continuing on down to the creek bed, if conditions permit. It takes a good 45 minutes of steady hiking to reach the Indian Kitchen canyon from the trailhead, and you will be retracing your route along the same trail to your entry point.

Next, drive over to **One Horse Gap** and tackle trail 106A. This forest trail has a more open feel with less underbrush and foliage along the path. The single-file dirt track, full of rocks and roots,

One Horse Gap

Indian Kitchen Trail, Lusk Creek Canyon Wilderness Area

continues steadily upward, and the usage by horseback riders is readily apparent. The climb is a little taxing, especially if you have just completed the Indian Kitchen Trail, but the distance is much shorter, and the view at One Horse Gap is amazing. Here you are, climbing through the forest, and suddenly, surprise! You reach a clearing with huge boulders and a picturesque narrow gap through the stone, big enough for only one horse at a time— hence the name. Hike on through the gap and reach the top of the bluff for another surprise. Wow! You are in a stone glade on top of the bluff with interesting sandstone rock formations to explore on a rather smooth level surface. There is a hitching area for horses and a fire ring for gathering around a campfire. When we were there in October, the trees were beautiful and the weather was flawless. It was worth every bit of effort to get there, and the trail back to the parking area is all downhill. It doesn't get any better than that!

Just so you know . . .

- If you are going to do this day trip as suggested, you will need to bring your own food and drink and plan on a picnic lunch at one of the areas. There are no concessions available in this area.

- **Lusk Creek Canyon's** main gorge is in a valley lined with cliffs of sandstone rising as much as 100 feet above Lusk Creek, a rocky stream flowing with several species of fish, including some that are rare in Illinois.

- The remains of a stone wall reputed to date from the Late Woodland period, A.D. 600–900, can be seen on the ridge above the steep bend in Lusk Creek Canyon.

- The **Indian Kitchen Trail** is in the middle of the 4,796-acre **Lusk Creek Canyon Wilderness Area**, dedicated as a nature preserve in 1970.

- Both Lusk Creek Canyon Wilderness Area and **One Horse Gap** can be enjoyed year-round with appropriate adjustments for weather conditions.

- For more information, stop at the Shawnee National Forest supervisor's office, on IL-145 south of Harrisburg, for site brochures and maps. Call 618-253-7114.

Riders at One Horse Gap

Day Trip	Landforms and Features	Distance (round-trip) and Duration	Difficulty	Facilities
Lusk Creek Canyon Wilderness Area Indian Kitchen Trailhead 37°30′21.42″ N 88°33′38.07″ W	Mature pine forest, massive sandstone cliff, rocky stream through a beautiful valley	Indian Kitchen Trail—3.5 miles, 3 hours	Moderate– difficult	Large parking area with privy (across the road from the trailhead gate)
One Horse Gap Trailhead parking 37°30′53.6″ N 88°27′10.3″ W	Mature second-growth mixed forest, massive sandstone boulders, narrow gap trail to top of bluff	Trail 106A—.75 mile, 1.5 hours	Moderate	Small parking area, no facilities

Barrens area at One Horse Gap

Directions

From Harrisburg to **Lusk Creek Canyon Wilderness Area**, take IL-145 south for 18 miles to Eddyville. Turn left (east) on County Road 5 (Eddyville Blacktop), going .3 mile to County Road 126. Turn left (north), as indicated by Indian Kitchen sign, continuing 1.5 miles to trailhead parking area on the left (west). Cross the road on foot to reach the trailhead gate.

From Lusk Creek to **One Horse Gap**, retrace route to Eddyville Blacktop, turn left (east), and continue for 9.7 miles to IL-146. Turn left (north) on IL-146 and continue for 4.1 miles. Turn left (north) on Lusk Road (One Horse Gap Blacktop), driving 4.4 miles to the "crossroads" intersection. There is a sign indicating a right turn (east) to One Horse Gap Lake, but you should continue straight ahead (north) for 1.8 miles to the One Horse Gap trailhead gate on the left (west) side of the road. For the last .3 of a mile, the road has large potholes, which may be impassable in wet weather. If that is the case, park at the pullout area for Forest Road 1667 and walk 250 yards north to the trailhead gate. The trailhead for 106A (One Horse Gap Trail) is within sight of the gate and is indicated by a wooden sign at the entrance of the trail.

Day Trip 7

Millstone Bluff

Rising 300 feet above the local valley, **Millstone Bluff** draws the eye and dominates the landscape for miles around. It is easy to see why the prehistoric people of the Mississippian culture decided to occupy this area. Visitors today have a wonderful opportunity to view the site of a largely undisturbed village dating from possibly A.D. 500–1500. Entering the trail from the parking area, you will immediately notice the large interpretive signs detailing information about the land and the Mississippian culture. Signs like these appear periodically along the trail route and are a major feature of this site. Millstone Bluff has, perhaps, the best signage of any of the natural places we have visited. Take the time to read the information and absorb the history as you climb the trail to the ancient village.

- Millstone Bluff
- Trigg Tower
- Jackson Falls

Trigg Tower

The trail leads steadily up through a quiet forest until it comes to the first of a series of wooden steps that will facilitate your climb to the site. Follow the signs to a short offshoot trail that will take you to a viewing platform for the sandstone petroglyph markings. The markings are faint and very difficult to see, but once again, the interpretive sign provides useful information. Retrace your route to the main trail and continue on up to the "residential" area on top of the bluff. Stand in this peaceful spot, and it will be easy to visualize where the homes must have been and to imagine children playing and adults going about their daily business. The trail loops around the perimeter of the village and then joins the original path for the descent to the parking area.

Take the time to stop at **Trigg Tower** as you continue toward your next major destination, Jackson Falls. Trigg Tower is next to the road, and a nice parking area makes it a convenient spot to pull over and make the climb to the viewing platform at the top of this old fire tower. You will have a panoramic view of the forest and valley from all directions.

Resume your journey to **Jackson Falls**, an area that is sure to be a highlight of any Shawnee Forest exploration. From the parking area, it is a short five-minute walk to the top of the bluff that is the falls area. You will be looking down into a sandstone rock glade. Don't be surprised if you see people on horseback, as this is a popular area for trail rides. To get down onto the valley floor, go left (south) at the falls and walk the path along the top of the bluff. It is a pleasant hike through trees and includes some natural stone "steps" as you gradually begin to descend. After about 20 minutes, you will cross a little creek, and then the path continues right (west) for 75 yards to a spot where you can climb down the rocks to the valley floor. It's about the only place where the rocks are situated to allow descent, but it is still a little daunting. We followed some young people down, and they had no trouble at all. Make note of where you descended as you will retrace this route out of the valley. Wander around and marvel at the sandstone boulders and huge cliffs that provide a challenge for rock climbers. It is quite common to see people rappelling in this area. Visit the falls from the bottom and linger among the rock formations. This is a challenging trip that can be accomplished in any season except during inclement winter weather.

Rock climbing at Jackson Falls

Signage at Millstone Bluff

Just so you know . . .

- **Millstone Bluff** is listed on the National Register of Historic Places.

- The prehistoric Mississippian village consists of about 24 house depressions arranged around a central plaza. A burial area from the same era is nearby.

- Early settlers used millstones carved from the bluff to mill farmers' grains into flour, giving the area its name.

- The 50-foot **Trigg Tower** has 70 steps leading to the top.

- **Jackson Falls** is extremely popular for rock climbers and is the only place within the Shawnee National Forest where this is permitted. No fees or permits are required to climb or camp here, but camping is limited to 14 days.

- It would be advisable to pack a lunch and carry water with you for this trip as there is no place to purchase food or drink and no drinkable water available at any of these places.

Jackson Falls

Day Trip	Landforms and Features	Distance (round-trip) and Duration	Difficulty	Facilities
Millstone Bluff 37°28′8.17″ N 88°41′20.85″ W	3-acre, 700-foot sandstone knob	1.5-mile loop trail, 1–1.5 hours	Moderate	Privy at parking area, interpretive signs and benches along trail
Trigg Tower 37°29′15.90″ N 88°44′10.08″ W	Climbable fire tower	30 minutes	Moderate	Parking area
Jackson Falls Campground 37°30′37.49″ N 88°40′54.99″ W	Scenic rocky glade, sandstone bluffs, freestanding boulders, medium waterfall	1.5–2 miles, 2–3 hours	Moderate–difficult	Privy at parking area, trailhead sign, primitive camping sites

Directions

To reach **Millstone Bluff** from Vienna, travel east on IL-146 for .3 mile to IL-147. Turn left (north) on IL-147 and drive 11.4 miles to the sign indicating the Millstone Bluff entrance. Turn left (north), as indicated by the sign, and go .3 mile to the parking area.

To reach **Trigg Tower** from Millstone Bluff, retrace route to the entrance, then turn right (west) on IL-147 and continue 3.8 miles to Trigg Tower Road, just before the village of Simpson. Turn right (north) on Trigg Tower Road and go 2.1 miles to the tower (at .6 mile stay right at the fork); turn right into the parking area.

To reach **Jackson Falls** from Trigg Tower, continue north on Trigg Tower Road for 1.9 miles until you reach a stop sign at Ozark Road. Turn right (east) on Ozark Road and go .1 mile to the Jackson Falls sign. Turn right (southeast) on this gravel road and continue for 1.9 miles to the parking area. A large sign indicates the Jackson Falls trailhead. If this parking area is full, cross the creek and continue along the rutted and bumpy road. There are additional campsites and pull-off places where you can park along this road. Vehicles with low clearance will need to be especially careful negotiating this road.

Day Trip 8

Old Stone Face

Old **Stone Face** can be hard to find. We almost gave up the first time we went looking for it but were pointed in the right direction by two young couples we met on the trail. Since then, we have learned that we are not the only people who have had difficulty coming face to face, so to speak, with this image of stone, deep in the Shawnee National Forest. You cannot see Old Stone Face from Stoneface Road or from the parking lot. You must make a rather strenuous half-mile hike up the cliff to a trail that goes along the cliff edge. From the parking lot, take the trail that runs east along the base of the cliff and keep going up, bearing right (south) at the fork, until you reach the trail at the top of the bluff. Continue going south. There are other scenic

- Old Stone Face
- Glen O. Jones Lake

overlooks that you will pass, looking northwest across the valley below, before you finally encounter Old Stone Face. Even though you know it is there, it is quite startling when you see it for the first time, and the view from this vantage point is striking.

At **Glen O. Jones Lake**, your next destination, follow the signs as you drive through the grounds. The bronze Chief Tecumseh statue stands at the entrance of the Cave Hill trailhead, one of four designated hiking trails at the lake. The arresting statue serves as a monument to this charismatic Shawnee chief, who must have been quite a man of vision with considerable insight into human nature: "If you see no reason for giving thanks, the fault is in yourself"; "Show respect to all people, but grovel to none"; and "Live your life so that the fear of death can never enter your heart," are some examples of his wisdom.

The Cave Hill Trail will take you past a small open meadow and into the forest and continues in an upward direction to the crest of a bluff. A short distance off the trail, at the edge of the cliff, you will find some sweeping, scenic overlooks. The cave, from which this trail derives its name, is no longer open to the public, but this is still a nice hike through an engaging forest. This is not a loop trail, so you will need to retrace your route to

Tecumseh statue, Glen O. Jones Lake

View of Glen O. Jones Lake

the Tecumseh statue. We turned around when the trail became progressively wilder and narrower and began to lead away from the bluff. Returning downhill, we noticed an offshoot trail to the south that led to a very nice rocky bluff overlook of a pretty little valley. From this point, it was a 20-minute hike back to the statue. The Lake Trail is another pleasant trail that begins at the campground parking area and continues around the lake. We have visited Glen O. Jones Lake many times, in various seasons, and have never found it to be overcrowded, making it another one of those well-kept secret "gems" of Southern Illinois.

Just so you know . . .

- Mead's milkweed, a species listed as threatened, grows in the **Old Stone Face** area, as do two other rare species: chokeberry and stonecrop.

- There is a large camping area for both tents and trailers and also a separate horse camping area at **Glen O. Jones Lake**, but electricity is not available. Hunting is restricted to posted areas. Check season dates and times at the park office. For information regarding the Saline County Wildlife and Conservation Area, call 618-276-4405.

- The Glen O. Jones Lake was named for a prominent Saline County state senator in the Illinois General Assembly.

- An area attraction is the **Pioneer Village Museum** at 1600 S. Feazel Street (south part of town), Harrisburg, with tours Tuesday through Sunday, 2:00–5:00 P.M. There is a small admission fee. Call 618-253-7342.

- Another possible side trip is a visit to **Old Shawnee-town** (23 miles east of Harrisburg on Route 13), home of Illinois's first state bank, an impressive four-story Greek structure with a five-columned portico. This floodplain village also has some picturesque old homes.

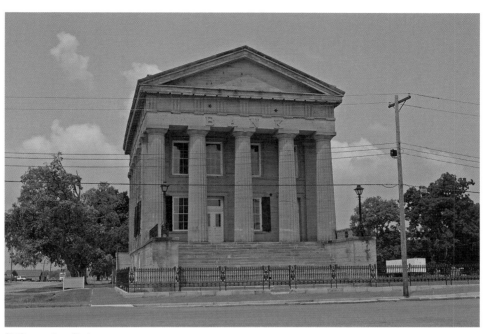

Old Shawneetown Bank

Day Trip	Landforms and Features	Distance (round-trip) and Duration	Difficulty	Facilities
Old Stone Face Parking area 37°39′39.7″ N 88°26′16.8″ W	Massive sandstone formation	1.5 miles, 1.5 hours	Moderate–difficult	Parking area
Glen O. Jones Lake Tecumseh parking area 37°41′29.9″ N 88°23′38.2″ W	105-acre lake, sandstone glades, forest trail	Cave Hill Trail— 3–4 miles, 2–3 hours

Lake Trail— 1.5 miles, 1.5 hours

Wildlife Trail— .25 mile, 30 minutes | Moderate–difficult

Easy

Easy | Restrooms, water, picnic tables, concession stand in season, boat rental, fishing, hunting, camping, horse campground |

Pioneer Village, Harrisburg

Directions

To reach **Old Stone Face** from Harrisburg, go south on IL-34 for 9 miles to the little village of Rudement. Turn left (east) at the Old Stone Face directional sign onto DeNeal Road (County Highway 5). Continue east on DeNeal Road for 4.3 miles. When you come to a T intersection, turn right (east) on Stoneface Road (follow Old Stone Face directional sign) and go 1 mile on this gravel road. Watch for a small Stoneface Lane sign. Turn right (south) on Stoneface Lane and go .3 mile to a circular drive parking lot. Stoneface Lane can be rough and heavily rutted.

To reach **Glen O. Jones Lake** from Old Stone Face, at Stoneface Lane entrance, turn right (east) onto the gravel Stoneface Road and continue 1.8 miles to a stop sign. Turn right (east) on Horseshoe Road (a blacktop road) and go 3 miles to another stop sign at a T junction. Turn right (south) on Forest Road. Go .4 mile to Eagle Creek Road, the entrance to Glen O. Jones Lake. There is a large brown Forest Service sign marking the entrance to the Saline County Wildlife and Conservation Area, the site of Glen O. Jones Lake. Follow signage within the park indicating campground parking, boat dock, trailheads, Tecumseh statue, and more.

The richness I achieve comes from Nature,
the source of my inspiration.
—Claude Monet

Day Trip 9

Hayes Creek Canyon

Start this day with an easy trek along an old forest road. You will see rocky bluffs on your right and will notice a Forest Service sign indicating that this is an ecological area, meaning it contributes significantly to the biodiversity of this habitat area. Continue to the right along the trail at the base of the bluff. You will be passing through a very pretty forest with interesting rock formations but nothing to indicate that you will soon see something really extraordinary. The trail winds downward a bit and then suddenly opens up to an unexpected view of the massive opening in the side of the bluff. This is **Sand Cave**. As you head upward to the mouth of the cave, you will have a very attractive view of the entrance, but you still will have no idea

- Sand Cave
- Jackson Hole
- Hayes Creek Canyon

Sand Cave

of the depth and sheer size of the chamber itself. Wow! This is not your everyday shelter cave but the top-of-the-line luxury model. The cave goes deep into the bluff with a level floor and a sense of spaciousness. This had to have been prime real estate for the Native Americans who were lucky enough to live here. Follow the bluff line north past the cave, and you will see other interesting rock formations. This is a truly unspoiled natural area, even though it gets regular usage by hikers and equestrians.

Equestrians are largely responsible for keeping many of the remote trails in Southern Illinois open for hikers to utilize. A good example of this is the **Jackson Hole** Trail. Enter at Horse Trail 497 on the right (west) side of the road. It is a short 10-minute hike to the horse tie-up area. From here, Jackson Hole is accessed only on foot. Follow the trail signs to the overlook into the small valley that is Jackson Hole. You will be standing on top of the falls. The trail continues north to a rock shelter and then begins to circle around the small glen containing the base of the lesser falls to your right (north). We found a spot to scramble down into the glen, but it wasn't easy, and coming back up at the same spot was harder than going down. From here, you will walk 100 feet to the main falls. You be the judge if you should descend. Retrace your route to the parking area.

Your last stop will be **Hayes Creek Canyon**. Enter at the privately owned Hayes Canyon Campground and make a brief stop at the camp office immediately to your right upon entering the grounds. Here you can ask questions and receive valuable information about the trails. This is a horse camp area, but there is a marked day-use parking location straight ahead from the office. Park and proceed on foot to a sign that says "All Traffic" and shows a red arrow pointing to the right. Turn as indicated and follow this road straight to a trail marker sign. Follow the arrow onto a narrow, rutted path obviously used by hikers and equestrians. The horse trail veers off to the right and goes above the stone glade that rims the canyon, but we walked along the stone glade with continuous views of the canyon. There is a clearly defined foot trail that leads you to an obvious stopping point where there is relatively easy access to the valley floor. This is a very scenic area. We visited during a dry time, but it would be easy to imagine flash flooding here during a wet season. Enjoy this beautiful, peaceful area and retrace your route to the parking lot.

Waterfall at Jackson Hole

Just so you know . . .

- **Sand Cave's** arched entrance and deep, dome-shaped room set it apart from the more typical shallow caves and sandstone shelter bluffs.

- Intersecting horse trails can be found around **Jackson Hole**, and a sign in the area indicates a path to the River-to-River Trail, 2.4 miles away.

- The **Hayes Canyon Campground** is a family-owned property next to the Shawnee National Forest, which caters to equestrians and offers access to the forest trails. For more information, contact Hayes Canyon Campground, PO Box 186, Main Street, Eddyville, IL, 62928, 618-672-4751, www.HayesCanyon.com.

- It would be advisable to pack a lunch and carry water with you on this trip as there is no place to purchase food or drink, other than light snacks at the Hayes Canyon Campground Office and Camp Store.

Hayes Creek Canyon

Jackson Hole

Day Trip	Landforms and Features	Distance (round-trip) and Duration	Difficulty	Facilities
Sand Cave Parking area 37°30′03.5″ N 88°38′35.9″ W	Among the largest sandstone caves in North America	1.5 miles, 1.5 hours	Easy	None
Jackson Hole Natural area 37°30′23.44″ N 88°36′54.10″ W	Sandstone cliffs, 50-foot waterfall	1.5 miles, 2 hours	Easy–difficult	None
Hayes Creek Canyon Office/store 37°30′40.6″ N 88°35′11.2″ W	Sandstone gorges, twin waterfalls 50 yards from campground, oak/hickory forest	Bluff Trail—1 mile, 1 hour	Easy–moderate	Hayes Canyon Campground has restrooms, information, and light concessions for sale

Directions

To reach **Sand Cave** from Vienna, travel east on IL-146 for .3 mile to IL-147. Turn left (north) on IL-147 and travel 12.5 miles to Cedar Grove Road (just prior to junction of IL-145). Turn left (north) on Cedar Grove Road and continue 3.7 miles to Sand Cave Road. Turn left (west) on Sand Cave Road and drive .2 mile to a grassy pull-off parking area with room for one or two cars. There is no sign marking the trailhead or the parking area, but the trail is actually an old road and is easy to see as you hike westward toward the cave.

To reach **Jackson Hole** from Sand Cave, retrace route to Cedar Grove Road. Turn left (north) on Cedar Grove Road and go 2.4 miles to a stop sign at Ozark Road. Turn right (east) on Ozark Road and go .4 mile to Mustang Lane. Turn right (south) on Mustang Lane and go .5 mile to a shallow pull-off area just prior to Horse Trail 497 on your right. Proceed on foot along Horse Trail 497 to Jackson Hole. Please note that Mustang Lane is fine for the first .2 mile but becomes a very bad, rutted lane road for the final .3 mile. Do not attempt to drive on this road with a low-clearance vehicle or in wet weather conditions. If you have a low-clearance vehicle or if the weather is poor, park your vehicle on a wide shoulder just prior to entering the noticeably narrower section of road and hike down to the trailhead. Respect private property on either side of the road.

To reach **Hayes Creek Canyon** from Jackson Hole, retrace route back to Ozark Road. Turn right (east) on Ozark Road and go 1.8 miles to Hayes Canyon Campground entrance. Turn right into Hayes Canyon Campground Office and Camp Store parking area.

To me a lush carpet of pine needles or spongy grass is
more welcome than the most luxurious Persian rug.
—*Helen Keller*

Day Trip 10

View of tunnel at Tunnel Hill State Trail

I f you prefer biking to hiking, do not miss the **Tunnel Hill State Trail**. Although many people use it as a hiking and dog walking trail, it is a stellar example of an easily accessible bike trail. Imagine a superhighway through a forest on an almost perfectly straight path and no worries about cars and trucks whizzing by. That's the Tunnel Hill State Trail, and it is heaven for pleasure bikers. If you are inclined toward extreme biking and testing your limits of strength and endurance, then this trail is probably not the challenge you want, but if you desire a pleasant day trip through gorgeous scenery without any big, demanding hills, then Tunnel Hill is a dream come true.

One of the great aspects of the Tunnel Hill State Trail is that there are many different places to get on or off, including at least

- Tunnel Hill State Trail

Breeden Trestle, Tunnel Hill State Trail

eight segments where trailheads and parking areas are offered. These entry and exit points are located in small towns along the route, and some include drinking water and privies in addition to parking access. It is not necessary to go the entire distance in order to have a great experience, but we heartily recommend it. A round trip in one day would be out of the question for most of us, but the 47.5-mile route from Harrisburg to the Henry N. Barkhausen Cache River Wetlands Center on Route 37 can be accomplished by a reasonably fit person, on a good bicycle, without resorting to the paramedics! You might consider doing what we did and have friends drop you off at one end and pick you up at the other.

The Tunnel Hill route is made from an abandoned railway system, last owned by Norfolk Southern Railroad, which granted the state of Illinois the right-of-way between Harrisburg and Karnak in 1991. The Illinois Department of Natural Resources (IDNR) then worked to develop the trail, using crushed limestone and gravel as surfacing material and installing privies and drinking fountains along the route. The railway trestle bridges are a unique feature of this trail, as is the 543-foot tunnel, located at its midpoint, for which the trail is named. You can see the end of the tunnel from the entrance, but the middle section becomes very dark (wearing sunglasses in the tunnel is not advised), and most bike riders begin to wobble and often dismount and walk rather than risk a crash. We have seen young people sail right through, though. Show-off kids!

For a short ride, the most popular segment of the trail seems to be the 9.3-mile stretch between Tunnel Hill and Vienna. This is a very scenic section that includes the famous tunnel as well as many of the trestle bridges, including the 90-foot-high Breeden Trestle. The Vienna Park includes the Tunnel Hill Site Office with modern restrooms, drinking water, ample parking, and easy access to food/concessions and lodging.

South from Vienna, you will enter the Cache River State Natural Area that culminates at the Barkhausen Cache River Wetlands Center, a wonderful facility with interactive wildlife displays that children especially will enjoy and a wealth of information about this region of southernmost Illinois. While you are on this part of your journey, watch for signs for Heron Pond, another great natural area that can be easily accessed from the trail.

Bike riders on Tunnel Hill State Trail

This is a bike trail to be savored at a relaxed pace while absorbing the peaceful natural habitat that surrounds you. Take a day off from routine and enter the realm of forest trees and heartland critters. This is an all-season trail, but fall is our favorite season for riding.

Trail Segments

- Harrisburg to Carrier Mills: 7.5 miles
- Carrier Mills to Stonefort: 6.7 miles
- Stonefort to New Burnside: 4.4 miles
- New Burnside to Tunnel Hill: 6.2 miles
- Tunnel Hill to Vienna: 9.3 miles
- Vienna to Belknap: 8 miles
- Belknap to Karnak: 2.8 miles
- Karnak to Barkhausen Cache River Wetlands Center: 2.5 miles

Tunnel Hill trail

Just so you know . . .

- The **Tunnel Hill State Trail** connects to several other trails, including the Trail of Tears National Historic Trail, with a site office and park in Vienna; the TransAmerica Bike Route (US Route 76); the American Discovery Trail; and the River-to-River Trail.

- The trail's surface is more suited for a mountain bike or hybrid without the narrow racing bike tires, but while it is not as hard a surface as pavement, it is generally solid with occasional soft places caused by weather conditions. A comfortable 2 percent grade runs the length of the trail.

- The IDNR worked to develop the trail from 1991 to 1998, when the first segment of the trail was opened. In the fall of 2001, a 2.5-mile trail spur from Karnak to the Barkhausen Cache River Wetlands Center was included.

- Species of trees along the trail include cypress and tupelo swamp trees, oak, hickory, cottonwood, and sweet gum. Animal species include bluebirds, killdeer, doves, quail, wild turkeys, squirrels, rabbits, raccoons, opossums, red foxes, and white-tailed deer. In the summer and early fall, keep an eye out for snakes.

- There are 23 trestles ranging in length from 34 to 450 feet. Breeden Trestle is the longest and also the highest at 90 feet.

- The Barkhausen Cache River Wetlands Center parking lot is accessible only when the building is open, so don't park there if you are going to finish your ride after regular business hours. Karnak is an alternate choice.

- No motorized vehicles, horses, hunting, or camping are allowed on the trail.

- The site office for Tunnel Hill State Trail is located on Route 146 on the east side of Vienna at the Vienna Park. Call the site office at 618-658-2168.

Tunnel Hill Biker

Day Trip	Landforms and Features	Distance (round-trip) and Duration	Difficulty	Facilities
Tunnel Hill State Trail Harrisburg parking area 37°43′13.1″ N 88°32′30.2″ W Tunnel Hill parking area 37°31′25.4″ N 88°50′18.2″ W	Refurbished RR bike/hiking trail made from crushed limestone and gravel	47.5 miles one way, 5–6 hours on bike	Easy–moderate	Restrooms, water, and parking at Harrisburg, Tunnel Hill, Vienna, and Karnak. The Tunnel Hill Site Office at Vienna has modern restrooms, brochures, a staffed office, and an exhibit area.

Directions

 To access the **Tunnel Hill State Trail** from Harrisburg, begin at the southern edge of Harrisburg, near the junction of Feazel Street and IL-45.

To access the Tunnel Hill State Trail from the Barkhausen Cache River Wetlands Center, take IL-146 from Vienna and go west for 5 miles to IL-37. Turn left (south) and continue for 9 miles, passing through the town of Cypress. Look for the Barkhausen Cache River Wetlands Center on the left (east) side of IL-37.

Western Region

One touch of nature makes the whole world kin.
—William Shakespeare

Day Trip 11

Heron Pond

L ocated within a floodplain in southernmost Illinois, the **Henry N. Barkhausen Cache River Wetlands Center** is in the perfect spot to serve as a focal point for exploring the beauty and diversity of the Southern Illinois region. Local citizens, government agencies, and environmental groups undertook a massive effort to make this great resource a reality, and the result is truly outstanding.

The 7,000-square-foot modern facility, owned and operated by the Illinois Department of Natural Resources, provides everything from maps and brochures to interactive exhibits and artifacts. Both children and adults will find this an informative and entertaining place. Start your visit by viewing the 12-minute

- Henry N. Barkhausen Cache River Wetlands Center

- Big Cypress Access

- Heron Pond

Barkhausen Cache River Wetlands Center

orientation video. This well-produced film provides an audiovisual overview of the Cache River locale with background information for those unfamiliar with the area. Wetlands staff are available to answer questions and acquaint you with the local flora and fauna. Linger at the wildlife viewing area and use the binoculars provided for an up-close look at life outdoors, including eagles, then go outside and walk the nature and hiking trails.

Now head over to **Big Cypress Access**, where you can see an amazing number of huge bald cypress trees, some of which are estimated to be over 1,000 years old. The entrance trail is obvious from the parking lot and provides easy access to the gigantic trees. You are sure to enjoy the staggering number of mature, old-growth trees in this small floodplain area. Several trails, often flooded during the wet season, branch out to all corners of this location, inviting exploration.

You absolutely must save time to visit **Heron Pond**, as it is one of the finest remaining cypress swamps in the state. Pick up a site brochure at the trailhead and follow the numbered signs along the path that correspond with information from the brochure. The trail itself is well defined and easy to walk but is not wheelchair accessible because of a bridge with a few stairs to climb.

The highlight of the trail is a modern boardwalk that provides easy access to the swamp's interior. As you walk among the ancient cypress trees, keep an eye out for great blue herons, eagles, black vultures, and beavers, all part of the diversity of animal and bird species within the wetlands. You might even see a river otter or bobcat and should always be aware that the poisonous cottonmouth/water moccasin is especially abundant here. Depending upon the season, you may notice a tiny pink swamp rose vine snaking up a cypress tree. Cypress bark acts as a deterrent to insects and diseases, thus nurturing the delicate swamp rose and allowing this scarce and fragile gem to exist in the Cache River swamps. Once off the boardwalk and back on the main trail, take the narrower quarter-mile offshoot, going left (west), to see the State Champion Cherrybark Oak; it is worth the extra effort. Heron Pond is most comfortably visited in the spring and the fall, but there is beauty here in all seasons.

Big Cypress Access

Just so you know . . .

- The **Henry N. Barkhausen Cache River Wetlands Center**, 8885 State Rt. 37, South Cypress, IL, 62923, is open Wednesday through Sunday, 9:00 A.M.–4:00 P.M. The center is wheelchair accessible, and there is no entrance fee. Call 618-657-2064 for more information.

- **Section 8 Woods Nature Preserve** (one mile south of the Wetlands Center on Route 37) features a 500-foot boardwalk leading into a bald cypress/water tupelo swamp. The **State Champion Water Tupelo** is 50 feet from the end of the boardwalk, toward the southeast. The preserve is wheelchair accessible.

- The **Lower Cache River Access Area** is another interesting side trip. From the Wetlands Center, turn left (south) on Route 37 for 200 yards and then turn right (west) on Perks Road. Continue west for 1.5 miles, turning left (south) on S. Quarry Road. Continue one mile to parking lot. Facilities here include a picnic shelter, toilets, drinking fountain, and a boat launching area. The **State Champion Bald Cypress** tree can be viewed from a platform at the end of a short hiking trail. Follow signs. The area is wheelchair accessible.

- **Big Cypress Access** is a hunter access area. For additional information, contact the site superintendent at the Cache River State Natural Area, 930 Sunflower Lane, Belknap, IL, 62908, 618-634-9678. Camping is not permitted.

- As with most areas of the Cache River State Natural Area, there is an enormous variety of plants, animals, birds, and reptiles at **Heron Pond**. Over 100 species have been listed as endangered or threatened. Rare and unusual plants include the sponge plant, copper iris, water elm, and American strawberry bush.

- No camping or hunting is allowed at Heron Pond.

- The current dimensions for the **State Champion Cherrybark Oak** are a circumference of 25 feet and a height of 103 feet.

Measuring the Illinois Champion Bald Cypress

Day Trip	Landforms and Features	Distance (round-trip) and Duration	Difficulty	Facilities
Barkhausen Cache River Wetlands Center Entrance gate 37°18′46.6″ N 89°01′15.9″ W	Lowland/swamp, modern nature center building, hiking trails	1-mile hike, 1.5–2 hours, including stop at visitor center	Easy	Restrooms, water, gift shop, museum, trails, Tunnel Hill State Trail access
Big Cypress Access Parking lot 37°18′33.6″ N 88°58′59.6″ W	Small swamp/floodplain, gigantic cypress trees	30 minutes	Easy	Parking area, hunting access
Heron Pond Parking lot 37°21′25.7″ N 88°54′47.1″ W	Cypress swamp/floodplain area	1.5-mile hike, 2 hours	Easy–moderate	Parking, privies, interpretive signs

Directions

To reach the **Henry N. Barkhausen Cache River Wetlands Center** from Vienna, take IL-146 west for 5 miles to IL-37. Turn left (south) on IL-37 and continue for 9 miles to the entrance, on your left.

To get to **Big Cypress Access** from the Wetlands Center entrance, turn left (south) on IL-37 and continue 1.7 miles to IL-169. Turn left (east) on IL-169 and go 2.2 miles to the Big Cypress sign at Karnak. Turn left (north), as the sign indicates, on Urbana Road and continue for 1.3 miles to the Big Cypress Access parking lot near the main road.

To get to **Heron Pond** from Big Cypress Access, retrace your route to IL-169, turn left (east), and continue for .5 mile (downtown Karnak). Turn left (north) on Belknap Road and travel for 5.3 miles to Heron Pond Road. Turn left (west) and continue for 1 mile to Heron Pond parking. The road comes to a dead end here.

Family fun at Section 8 Woods Nature Preserve boardwalk

*Geographically speaking, there is perhaps no position
in the whole of the United States which would promise
better for the site of a large city than that of Cairo.*
—*Lieutenant-Colonel Arthur Cunynghame*

Day Trip 12

A. B. Stafford Memorial Library, Cairo

et us just say right from the start, we like **Cairo**. You get
the feeling of having stepped back in time when you drive
through the old downtown district with its crumbling buildings
on the one hand and beautiful historic church buildings on the
other. And, yes, that back-in-time feeling can quickly become
an uneasy feeling as you notice boarded-up storefronts and the
living conditions in some neighborhoods. Still, this town is fascinating because of its prominence in the past, and although it
has been plagued with problems, the glory days can be witnessed
in some of the remaining public buildings and in the historic
district, where there are mansions and homes that rival those
in any genteel southern city.

- Cairo
- Mound City National Cemetery
- Horseshoe Lake State Fish and Wildlife Area

Mound City National Cemetery

Two places you must visit are the A. B. Stafford Memorial Library and the Custom House Museum, an easy walk across the street from each other on the main intersection through town. The minute you step into the library, you feel surrounded by the rarified atmosphere of old books and historical documents. This library, established in 1883, is a beautiful example of Queen Anne architecture, featuring stained glass, ornate woodwork, antiques (including a rare Tiffany grandfather clock), a 200-seat auditorium, paintings, a large collection of Civil War records, and numerous books and periodicals. Cross the road and tour the Custom House Museum, an impressive three-story brick building completed in 1872 as a port of delivery where goods being transported from New Orleans were inspected and fees on those goods were collected. The restored building opened as a museum in 1984 and houses Civil War memorabilia, an old-time general store, a drug store, a USS gunboat replica, antiques, and more. Next, take a tour of Magnolia Manor, an impeccably maintained mansion in the historic district, and then drive south all the way through town to Fort Defiance State Park, where the blue waters of the Ohio River and the muddy waters of the Mississippi River converge at the southernmost point in

Illinois. Spend some time watching the river traffic go by and realize that at one time, this area was teeming with steamboats and Civil War activity.

Now drive to another place of historical significance from the Civil War era, the **Mound City National Cemetery**, one of 12 original national cemeteries. In 1874, the state of Illinois donated a monument commemorating the soldiers and sailors of Illinois who had served in the Civil War. This monument stands in the center of the cemetery as a focal point among the rows of white marble headstones that mark the graves. National cemeteries are reserved for those who served in the US military; however, there are 47 Confederate burials of those who died as prisoners of war. Every American war since the Mexican–American War (1846–48) is represented among the burials. The lodge building, containing Civil War memorabilia and pictures of local area history, has been placed on the National Register of Historic Places and is open to the public. The grounds are meticulously groomed, reflecting the attitude of respect and honor due our military servicemen and servicewomen.

Complete your day by taking a drive around **Horseshoe Lake State Fish and Wildlife Area** near the town of Olive Branch.

Horseshoe Lake

The main purpose of the lake is to provide refuge for waterfowl, but it also serves as a significant bird-watching site and offers numerous recreational activities. It has been aptly stated that with the predominance of bald cypress and tupelo trees, this area looks more like a Louisiana bayou than a lake in Illinois. Drive slowly around the lake and see if you can spot a huge bald eagle nest cradled in the top of a bald cypress tree. This is a trip you can take at any time of the year, but the eagles' nests are most easily spotted in winter.

Just so you know . . .

- The public **A. B. Stafford Memorial Library** is at 1606 Washington Avenue, Cairo. Hours are Monday–Friday, 10:00 A.M.–5:00 P.M. There is no admission fee. Call 618-734-1840 for information.

- The Cairo **Custom House Museum** is at 1400 Washington Avenue. There is no entrance fee, but donations are suggested. The museum is maintained by volunteers, and hours vary. Call 618-734-9632 for information.

- **Magnolia Manor** is a 14-room brick mansion built in 1869 by Charles A. Galigher. Located at 2700 Washington Avenue in Cairo's historic district, the mansion has been owned and operated by the Cairo Historical Society since 1952. President Ulysses S. Grant reportedly stayed at the mansion after his term as president. Magnolia Manor is open daily, 9:00 A.M.–5:00 P.M. (1:00–5:00 P.M. on Sunday). There is an admission fee. Call 618-734-0201 for tour information.

- **Fort Defiance State Park** is two miles south of Cairo on Highway 51. The spring flood of 2011 heavily damaged this area, and it has not reopened as of this writing. Call 618-734-4127 for information.

- The military headstones at the **Mound City National Cemetery** are white marble and rounded on top and are

Custom House Museum, Cairo

42 inches long, 13 inches wide, and 4 inches thick. More than 2,600 unknowns are buried here. Headstones with gabled or pointed tops indicate the Confederate burials. Located at the junctions of Highways 37 and 51, the cemetery is open daily from sunrise to sunset. There is no admission fee. Call 618-784-9041 for information.

- At the **Mound City Marine Ways** on the Mound City riverfront, the rails from which the ironclad gunboats were launched into the Ohio River during the Civil War are still visible.

- There is a 12.3-mile biking trail at **Horseshoe Lake**.

- For information about Horseshoe Lake, contact the site superintendent at Horseshoe Lake State Fish and Wildlife Area, Miller City, IL, 62962, 618-776-5689.

Day Trip	Landforms and Features	Distance (round-trip) and Duration	Difficulty	Facilities
Cairo A. B. Stafford Memorial Library 37°00′12.1″ N 89°10′24.2″ W	Founded in 1837, southernmost Illinois city, steeped in history	2 miles in and around town, 3–4 hours	Easy	Food, water, restrooms, shops, wheelchair accessible
Mound City National Cemetery Parking area 37°05′13.8″ N 89°10′42.0″ W	Established in 1864, over 9,000 military burials	30 minutes–1 hour to stroll cemetery	Easy	Restrooms, water, gift shop in caretaker's lodge, wheelchair accessible
Horseshoe Lake Picnic area at spillway 37°06′32.6″ N 89°19′31.3″ W	2,400-acre lake resembling a Louisiana bayou	30 minutes–1 hour to drive around lake and stop at a few observation points	Easy	Picnicking, camping, boating, fishing, hunting, hiking/biking trails

Directions

From Marion to **Cairo**, take I-57 south for 52 miles to Exit 1. Go east on IL-3 for 1 mile to the junction with IL-37. Turn right (south), continuing for 2 miles to Cairo.

From Cairo to **Mound City National Cemetery**, go north on US 51/IL-37 for 4 miles to the entrance of the cemetery.

From Mound City National Cemetery entrance to **Horseshoe Lake**, turn right (west) and go 100 yards to US 51. Turn right (northwest) and continue for 2.5 miles to County Road 6 (Olive Branch Road) at the north edge of Mounds. Turn left (west) on Olive Branch Road and continue for 4.7 miles, where CR 6 becomes IL-3. Continue west on IL-3 for 2.5 miles to East Side Drive and turn left (south), which is the beginning point of a 17-mile loop around Horseshoe Lake. After a stop at the spillway park, continue west for .5 mile to West Side Drive. Turn right (north) and continue for 3.7 miles to Miller City Road. At Miller City T road, turn right (north) toward the village of Olive Branch, which is on IL-3.

*Once you have heard the lark, known the swish of
feet through hill-top grass and smelt the earth made
ready for the seed, you are never again going to be
fully happy about the cities and towns that man
carries like a crippling weight upon his back.*
—Gwyn Thomas

Day Trip 13

Green Earth: Chautauqua Bottoms Nature Preserve

Visitors to the city of Carbondale have several options for interesting and unique outdoor activities. We highly recommend a visit to one or more of the **Green Earth Nature Preserves** and a stop at the **Marberry Arboretum** near the Southern Illinois University campus.

As stated in its publications, Green Earth, Inc. is a not-for-profit corporation that was established in 1974 to acquire, preserve, and provide public access to natural areas in Carbondale. This group does a wonderful job fulfilling its stated mission. It is an unexpected delight to find nature trails of this quality and variety within the confines of the metropolitan area. Each site is marked with a large Green Earth Nature Preserve sign at the

- Green Earth
  Nature Preserves
  - Brush Hill Nature
    Preserve
  - Oakland Nature
    Preserve
  - Chautauqua Bottoms
    Nature Preserve
  - Fernlands Nature
    Preserve
- Marberry
  Arboretum

Green Earth: Fernlands Trail

parking area. Stop at the trailhead and pick up an informational brochure specific to the area you are about to explore.

Each of the four areas we mention has unique features and characteristics. The trails are well marked, relatively short, and of easy to moderate difficulty. It is certainly possible to visit all four areas in one day, or you may choose to linger in one or more areas. Our favorites include the Stan Harris Trail at the **Oakland Nature Preserve** and the Fernlands Trail at the **Fernlands Nature Preserve**. The Stan Harris Trail is a short loop that meanders through prairie grass, flowers in season, a low-lying wooded area, and an oak/hickory forest. The variety of natural species available in such a small area is remarkable. The Oakland Nature Preserve also includes a one-acre tall grass prairie that is easily viewed from the parking area and the Woodland Trail, just north of the parking area. You can park your vehicle and access all three areas from one location. The Fernlands Nature Preserve features a very nice woodland hike, a little longer and a bit more difficult than the Stan Harris Trail, containing an abundance of ferns throughout the lowland areas. In all four places that make up the Green Earth Nature Preserves, the brochures provided at the trailheads contain much valuable information about the various plant life and natural features that can be observed during your hike.

The Marberry Arboretum is a pleasant place to take a stroll and try to identify many of the rare and unusual plants that William Marberry, a botany teacher and world traveler, collected from such places as India, China, and Burma and many countries in Europe. Enjoy the unpaved hiking path that winds uphill and downhill through forested areas and open meadows, with picnic tables and benches conveniently situated along the way.

The Green Earth Nature Preserves and the Marberry Arboretum may be enjoyed at any season of the year but especially from spring through fall, when you will catch flowers in bloom.

Red buckeye tree, Marberry Arboretum

Just so you know . . .

- The **Green Earth Nature Preserves** are open to the public year-round from dawn to dusk. Dumping, camping, or removal of any plants or animals is strictly prohibited. Funding is dependent almost entirely on donations. For more information, visit www.greenearthinc.org or contact the Green Earth executive director at PO Box 441, Carbondale, IL, 62903, 618-201-3774.

- Green Earth has one half-time employee, the executive director, and is governed by a volunteer board that meets monthly to discuss property management and governance issues.

- The **Marberry Arboretum** is maintained by the Carbondale Park District and is home to more than 100 genera, 600 species, and 20,000 plants.

- The SIU campus offers an accessible, 2.2-mile paved path along the shores of **Campus Lake**. Visitors can walk or run or participate in numerous exercise challenges, including a rope and wall climb, which are located just off the path.

- The **University Museum**, on the SIU campus, is open Tuesday–Friday, 10:00 A.M.–4:00 P.M., and Saturday and Sunday, 1:00–4:00 P.M. The museum is closed on Mondays, holidays and university breaks. Admission is free, and the museum is wheelchair accessible. For more information, visit www.museum.siu.edu or call 618-453-5388.

Day Trip	Landforms and Features	Distance (round-trip) and Duration	Difficulty	Facilities
Green Earth Nature Preserves Parking areas	Hiking trails through various habitats			
Brush Hill 37°42′41.4″ N 89°11′53.4″ W	Upland and lowland forest	1 mile, 1 hour	Moderate	Parking area, trailhead sign
Oakland 37°44′26.8″ N 89°13′39.4″ W	Forest and prairie habitat	Stan Harris Trail— .5 mile, 30 minutes Woodland Trail— .5 mile, 30 minutes	Easy Easy	Parking area, trailhead sign
Chautauqua Bottoms 37°42′57.8″ N 89°14′39.2″ W	Bottomland hardwood forest, native prairie grasses and forbs, three trails	1 mile, 1 hour	Easy	Parking area, trailhead sign
Fernlands 37°41′11.6″ N 89°15′44.6″ W	Moist woodland habitat featuring clear streams, mosses, ferns, and spring wildflowers	.8 mile, 1 hour	Moderate	Parking area, trailhead sign
Marberry Arboretum Parking area 37°42′00.4″ N 89°12′33.7″ W	25-acre arboretum	.75-mile hiking trail, 1 hour	Moderate	Parking area, benches, picnic tables

Directions

To get to the **Brush Hill Nature Preserve**, begin at the intersection of US-51 and IL-13 in Carbondale. Travel east on IL-13 for .5 mile to Wall Street. Turn right (south) on Wall Street and continue for .6 mile to E. Park Street. Turn left (east) on E. Park Street and go .7 mile to the parking area on the right (west) side of the road. A Green Earth sign marks the trailhead. The parking lot is next door to a Carbondale fire station.

To get to the **Oakland Nature Preserve**, begin at the intersection of US-51 and IL-13 in Carbondale. Travel west on IL-13 for .5 mile, turning right (north) on Oakland Avenue. Continue for 1 mile to the parking area on the east side of the road. (Note: This 1-mile stretch of Oakland follows a zigzag pattern. Keep left at W. Willow and keep right at Rigdon, and then you will be back on Oakland Avenue.) A Green Earth sign marks the trailhead.

To reach the **Chautauqua Bottoms Nature Preserve**, begin at the intersection of US-51 and IL-13 in Carbondale. Travel west on IL-13 for 1.4 miles, turning left (south) on Emerald Lane. Travel south on Emerald Lane for 1 mile to Chautauqua Road. Turn right (west) and continue for approximately 200 yards to the entrance sign marking the parking area on the right (north) side of the road.

To get to the **Fernlands Nature Preserve**, begin at the intersection of US-51 and IL-13 in Carbondale. Travel south on US-51 for 1.8 miles to Pleasant Hill Road. Turn right (west) on Pleasant Hill Road and travel 1.5 miles to Union Hill Road. Turn left (south) on Union Hill Road and travel 1.3 miles to Kennedy Road. Turn right (west) and travel .3 mile to the parking area on the left (south) side of the road.

To reach the **Marberry Arboretum**, begin at the Pleasant Hill Road intersection in Carbondale. Turn left (east) onto Pleasant Hill Road and drive .6 mile to the Marberry Arboretum entrance and parking area on the right (south) side of the road.

Rothrock Prairie at Oakland Nature Preserve

Day Trip 14

Shelter cave, Cedar Lake

In its entirety, the **Cedar Lake Trail System** south of Murphysboro totals 15 miles, but for the perfect day hike, we recommend starting at the Cove Hollow trailhead and hiking that section all the way to the Wolf Den Hollow Loop and continuing on to Boat Dock Road, where there is a small parking area directly across from the spot where you will exit the trail. This option works best if someone drops you off at the Cove Hollow trailhead and picks you up on Boat Dock Road. If you follow this suggestion, you will be hiking more than four miles of terrain that features spectacular rock shelters and rock walls formed from the sandstone bluffs, views of the lake, scenic overlooks, and a hardwood forest.

- Cedar Lake Trail System
- Bald Knob Cross

For shorter outings, you could park at the Cove Hollow trail-head, take the brief hike down to the shelter bluff, a prime example of a Native American habitation area, and then return to the trailhead parking lot. The main trail goes downhill, east toward the lake, and then turns southwest above the lakeshore. Cove Hollow is a rocky hollow at the end of an inlet of Cedar Lake. The lake will be below on your left, with cliffs on the right.

After returning to the parking lot, drive to Route 127, turn left (south), and continue half a mile to Boat Dock Road (directly across the road from the Pomona Natural Bridge sign). Turn left (east) on Boat Dock Road, travel for .7 mile, and park at the access area on the south side of the road. Cross the road to enter the Wolf Den Hollow Loop Trail. Hike for about a mile to the Wolf Den Hollow area, a series of rocky overhangs that provide shelter for animals, then retrace your route to your vehicle.

Brochures available from the Mississippi Bluffs Ranger District provide a detailed map of the entire Cedar Lake Trail System that will help you visualize how these trails are connected and their general proximity to the lake. We recommend picking up one of these maps prior to starting your hike. The dirt trails are narrow but well defined, and the forest is lovely for hiking year-round. Be aware of hunters during hunting season, and keep

Cove Hollow Trail, Cedar Lake

alert for snakes and poison ivy. However you choose to proceed, you will enjoy this hike through a beautiful forested area offering a variety of scenic views.

From Cedar Lake, it is a short drive south on Route 127 to the picturesque village of Alto Pass. This is the access point for the road to Bald Knob Mountain and the majestic cross, a towering steel structure covered with white porcelain panels. Follow the directional signs to the Bald Knob Mountain summit, driving along a winding, scenic all-weather road to the entrance gates, which are open from sunrise to sunset each day. From here, it is a short distance to the visitor center perched on the edge of a bluff, from which you can look over the forested valley below. The **Bald Knob Cross** will be in full view and is only a short walk uphill from the visitor center parking lot. Beneath the cross, you will enjoy a panoramic outlook. You will be standing on one of the most prominent elevations in Southern Illinois as you gaze across the Illinois Ozarks, approximately 50 miles north of the confluence of the Mississippi and Ohio Rivers. Be sure to stop in the visitor center and learn some of the history of the cross's construction and about the many people who contributed to the completion of this great landmark in Southern Illinois. This is a "must see" destination any time of the year.

Bald Knob Cross

Wolf Den Hollow, Cedar Lake Trail System

Just so you know . . .

- **Cedar Lake** is the water source for the city of Carbondale.

- Private lands border the northern portion of Cedar Lake, but the entire southern half of the lake is surrounded by Shawnee National Forest land.

- Four trailheads provide access to the **Cedar Lake Trail System**: Little Cedar Loop, Cove Hollow, Wolf Den Hollow, and the River-to-River Trail segment.

- For more information about Cedar Lake, call the Mississippi Bluffs Ranger District at 618-833-8576.

- **Bald Knob Cross** stands 111 feet tall, and its arms span 63 feet. When illuminated at night, it can be seen over an area of 7,500 square miles.

- In addition to the annual Easter sunrise service, special yearly events include the Blessing of the Bikes on the last Sunday in April; Bar-B-Que during the second weekend in September; Union County Color Fest during the second weekend in October; and Fall Festival during the third weekend in October.

Quetil Trail, Alto Pass

- For information on Bald Knob Cross, call 618-893-2344, email info@baldknobcross.com, or visit www.baldknobcross.com.

- For a spectacular long-distance view of the cross, drive east through Alto Pass and take the road that leads from Alto Pass to Cobden (Skyline Drive). Stop at the very nice picnic shelter on the rocky cliff top (approximately 300 yards east of downtown Alto Pass) and enjoy one of the best views in Southern Illinois as you gaze across the forested valley to Bald Knob Cross.

- From the cliff-top picnic shelter, look for the hidden stone staircase that leads down to the **Quetil Trail**, an easy foot and bicycle trail that follows the old railroad grade along the base of the cliff. The trailhead is at the east edge of "downtown" Alto Pass, near an ample parking area complete with picnic table.

- The **Root Beer Saloon**, 4 Main Street, Alto Pass, serves sandwiches, soup, desserts, and soda fountain root beer, as well as homemade fudge. The unusual decor of the building is worth a visit, and we highly recommend the seafood gumbo. Call 618-893-1634 for information.

Day Trip	Landforms and Features	Distance (round-trip) and Duration	Difficulty	Facilities
Cedar Lake Trail System	1,750-acre lake			Cedar Lake offers fishing, boating, canoeing, swimming, and primitive camping. This is also an access area for hunters. Cove Hollow trailhead has a small parking lot. Pomona Boat Launch, at the dead end of Boat Dock Rd., has a large parking area, accessible restroom, boat launch, and trailer parking.
Cove Hollow trailhead parking 37°38′23.8″ N 89°17′27.9″ W	Rugged trail, sandstone boulders and bluffs, shelter cave, hardwood forest	Cove Hollow Trail to Boat Dock Rd.— 4.5 miles (one way), 2.5 hours	Moderate– difficult	
Wolf Den Hollow Trail entrance on Boat Dock Rd. 37°37′24.9″ N 89°18′42.0″ W		Wolf Den Hollow Trail from Boat Dock Rd.— 2 miles, 1 hour	Moderate	
Bald Knob Cross Parking area 37°33′04.4″ N 89°20′51.4″ W	111-foot white porcelain steel structure atop Bald Knob Mountain, outstanding vistas	.25 mile, 30 minutes to walk around and view cross	Easy	Wheelchair accessible visitor center has restrooms, snacks, water, and gift shop.

Directions

From Murphysboro to **Cedar Lake's** Cove Hollow trailhead, go south on IL-127 for 9 miles. Turn left (east) on County Road 17 (Dutch Ridge Road) and continue east for 1.2 miles to Cove Hollow Road. Turn right (east) onto Cove Hollow Road and continue for 1 mile. The road comes to a dead end at the Cove Hollow trailhead parking area.

From Cedar Lake, retrace road to IL-127. Turn left (south) on IL-127 and continue for 5 miles to Alto Pass and the **Bald Knob Cross** sign. Follow the signs to Bald Knob Cross, which is 4.3 miles west of Alto Pass.

Look deep into nature, and then you
will understand everything better.
—Albert Einstein

Day Trip 15

Big Rocky Hollow Trail, Ferne Clyffe State Park

In 1923, Miss Emma Rebman's property was named the most beautiful spot in Illinois, according to a plaque marking the entrance to Rebman Trail. On Sundays, the public was allowed to visit for a 10-cent admission fee. Today, visitors may enjoy **Ferne Clyffe State Park** any day of the week, and admission is free. The plaque in the park is dedicated to Rebman, who owned 140 acres of the property and wished to see the area preserved as a state park. In 1929, Rebman offered to sell the land to the state of Illinois, but it wasn't until 1949 that the sale was completed. Today, the park has expanded to include 2,430 acres and is visited by a quarter of a million people each year. Emma Rebman would undoubtedly be proud.

- Ferne Clyffe State Park
- Cedar Bluff
- Bork's Waterfall

Hawk's Cave Trail, Ferne Clyffe State Park

There are 18 trails to choose from at Ferne Clyffe, but two of the most popular are Hawk's Cave Trail and Big Rocky Hollow Trail. These trails are perfect for the first-time or day trip visitor and will provide a sense of the geological features of the park and a taste of the abundant plant life, including the ferns that thrive here and give the park its name.

Hawk's Cave Trail is an easy, one-mile loop that features a 150-foot-long shelter bluff. The trail winds through a forested area brimming with plant life on either side of the narrow path as it heads upward toward the shelter bluff, leading past the shelter cave and looping through the forest until it rejoins the original path back to the trailhead. The Big Rocky Hollow Trail is probably the most popular trail at Ferne Clyffe. It provides an easy hike through a narrow canyon of rocky bluffs on both sides and terminates at a 100-foot-tall intermittent waterfall. During wet seasons of the year, this is a spectacular sight. The entire approach is very scenic and is on mostly level ground. Families with young children will find this to be an accessible trail, and opportunities for taking outstanding photographs abound at the waterfall. Bring a picnic lunch, and take the time to explore as many of the trails as you can.

In 1995, the Illinois Department of Natural Resources and the US Forest Service finalized a land trade that resulted in the Cedar Bluff/Draper Bluff area being added to the Ferne Clyffe State Park for management as a land and water reserve. From the main park area at Ferne Clyffe, drive over to **Cedar Bluff** and hike the Cedar Bluff Trail. A moderate half-mile loop hike leads to a scenic vista atop Cedar Bluff. You will have a sweeping, panoramic view of the valley below. From here, we suggest you retrace your route to the parking area, but it is possible to take a longer, two-mile trail that continues from the vista along the ridgetop and then descends the bluff and intersects with Bobcat Loop Trail. Make sure you have a good map of the area and stay on the marked trail. Only foot access is allowed. Or you can skirt the base of the bluff and drive along Cedar Grove Road to other access points for trailheads, such as **Bork's Waterfall** Trail. Bork's Waterfall is an area of Ferne Clyffe State Park that is less well known than the main waterfall at Big Rocky Hollow Trail but is a short and easy walk from the parking area and equally photogenic. This less crowded area features the approximately

Bork's Waterfall

Narrow rock passage at Ferne Clyffe

45-foot falls dropping into a small canyon with bluffs on either side. The crest of the falls is completely open, with no barriers or railings, so use extreme caution at this approach.

There are so many unique areas to visit within the confines of Ferne Clyffe State Park that you are certain to encounter thrilling scenery. The rock formations are wonderful any time of year, and the woodland wildflowers provide gorgeous groundcover in the spring. In the fall, the tree foliage is a lovely mix of autumn splendor. Is this the most beautiful spot in Illinois? You be the judge.

Just so you know . . .

- George Rogers Clark and his expedition reportedly passed through or near **Ferne Clyffe** on their trip to Fort Kaskaskia in 1778.

- There are more than 700 species of plant life to be found in **Ferne Clyffe State Park** and the 53-acre **Round Bluff Nature Preserve**. Woodland wildflowers include

Winter hiking at Cedar Bluff

Dutchman's breeches, trillium, spring beauty, and trout lily. Tree species include flowering dogwood, redbud, serviceberry, spicebush, sumac, sweet gum, maple, oak, and hickory. All plants and animals within the preserve are protected by law.

- The 16-acre **Ferne Clyffe Lake** is open to bank fishing, but boating and swimming are prohibited. Fish species include largemouth bass, bluegill, and channel catfish.

- The River-to-River Trail passes through Ferne Clyffe State Park over eight miles of moderately difficult terrain.

- For more information about Ferne Clyffe State Park, write to PO Box 10, Goreville, IL, 62939, or call 618-995-2411.

- **Cedar Bluff's** cliff walls average 80–90 feet and include several rock shelters.

Day Trip	Landforms and Features	Distance (round-trip) and Duration	Difficulty	Facilities
Ferne Clyffe State Park Entrance gate 37°31′56.9″ N 88°58′00.0″ W	Impressive rock formations, bluffs, canyons, rock shelters, water-falls, and small streams	Hawk's Cave Trail—1 mile, 1 hour	Easy	Campgrounds for every type of camper: modern, primitive, youth group, backpack, or equestrian; 18 hiking trails; 7 picnic areas with tables, grills, parking, and toilets; hunting in 1,750 acres of forested habitat
		Big Rocky Hollow Trail—1 mile, 1 hour	Easy	
		Ferne Clyffe Lake Trail—1 mile, 1 hour	Easy	
		Blackjack Oak Trail—2 miles, 1.5 hours	Moderate	
Cedar Bluff Trailhead on Cedar Grove Church Rd. 37°30′57.9″ N 89°01′25.5″ W	Massive sand-stone bluffs and boulders, dry up-land forest of oak/hickory and red cedar, outstanding scenic vista	Cedar Bluff Trail—.5-mile loop to scenic vista, 30 minutes	Moderate	Small parking area, trailhead sign
Bork's Waterfall Trail parking area 37°32′29.4″ N 89°01′19.4″ W		Bork's Waterfall Trail—.25 mile, 30 minutes	Easy	Small parking area, trailhead sign

Directions

To **Ferne Clyffe State Park** from downtown Marion, take IL-37 south for 12 miles to Goreville. Continue south on IL-37 from Goreville for 1.5 miles to the Ferne Clyffe State Park entrance. Turn right (west) and follow directional signs for 1.75 miles to the main parking area.

From the Ferne Clyffe State Park entrance to **Cedar Bluff**, turn right (south) onto IL-37 and travel 4.4 miles to Buncombe. Turn right (west) on Main Street, which becomes Lick Creek Road. Drive 5 miles to Cedar Grove Road. Turn right (north) and go .7 mile to the Cedar Grove Church. Take the right (east) fork for .3 mile, uphill, to the small parking area off the left side of the road. There is a sign marking the Cedar Bluff Trail, just inside the trailhead entrance.

To reach **Bork's Waterfall** from Cedar Bluff Trail parking, retrace route to the Cedar Grove Church. Turn right (north) on Cedar Grove Road/Regent Lane and continue for 3 miles to a marked parking area on your right. Follow the obvious trail to the waterfall. When water is flowing, you can see and hear the waterfall from the parking area.v

Nature is the art of God.
—Thomas Browne

Day Trip 16

Balanced Rock, Giant City State Park

Youth groups picnicking under the shelters, families arranging food on picnic tables while children swing on nearby playground equipment, college students tossing a Frisbee—these are scenes from **Giant City State Park** on any given summer day. This multiuse park attracts more than a million visitors annually, and for good reason. The natural beauty of this setting is unsurpassed, and it is easily accessed from Carbondale or Makanda. For the day visitor, the highlight of the visit is hiking one or more of the many wonderful trails. You may choose to walk the Giant City Nature Trail, possibly the most popular in the park, which takes you through the "Giant City Streets" lined by huge bluffs of sandstone. You will squeeze through some narrow alleyways, and the terrain can be rough, so always watch your footing. There are steps to climb and bridges to cross but also benches for the weary.

- Giant City
  State Park

Indian Creek Nature Trail is another popular choice, which takes you to a shelter bluff showing signs of human habitation from thousands of years ago. The Post Oak Trail, specially designed for disabled visitors, runs along the top of a bluff, offering wonderful views for those with physical limitations. Even so, this trail may not be negotiable by someone in a wheelchair unless accompanied by an able-bodied person. Our favorite is Trillium Trail, not far from the main entrance to the park near Makanda. This loop trail takes you past gorgeous sandstone bluffs on the lower part and continues to wind upward, past marvelous spring flowers if you are visiting in that season, to a set of steep wooden steps. At the top of the steps, turn right. You will be on top of the bluff and will pass through a dry forest area as you continue along the bluff top. You will notice some expansive views of neighboring bluffs across the road. Stay on the trail as it winds back down to the Trillium Trail parking area.

Redbuds in bloom, Giant City State Park

Before going on any of the trails, though, we recommend stopping at the visitor center to receive trail maps and learn a bit of the history of the park, which covers over 4,000 acres. Also, don't miss a visit to the Giant City Lodge, a well-preserved 1930s

structure with a large dining room serving excellent, reasonably priced food. Near the lodge parking lot, climb to the observation deck of the water tower, 50 feet up, and enjoy a spectacular view of the surrounding area.

October is a wonderful month to visit as the weather is generally mild, the color is spectacular, and pesky summer insects are no longer a problem. Spring brings lovely flowering trees and a unique display of flowers along Trillium Trail and elsewhere in the park. In any season, Giant City is renowned for its splendor and is a "must see" destination.

Devil's Stand Table, Giant City State Park

Just so you know . . .

- The **Giant City Lodge** serves breakfast, lunch, and dinner daily. Cabins with forest views are available for overnight guests. None of the cabins has kitchen facilities, and pets are not allowed. The lodge is closed each year from early December to early February. For lodge and cabin reservations, call 618-457-4921 or write to Giant City Lodge, 460 Giant City Lodge Road, Makanda, IL, 62958.

- **Giant City Stables**, located in the park, offers guided rides, weather permitting. The stables are open from March 15 to October 31 each year but are closed on Tuesdays. Call 618-529-4110 for information.

- For fishing and boating information for nearby **Crab Orchard Lake**, contact Crab Orchard Wildlife Refuge, part of the US Fish and Wildlife Service, at 618-997-3344.

- The **Class A campground** provides water, electricity, showers, and sanitary facilities for tent and trailer camping. There are 85 Class A campsites, and reservations may be made in advance. The **Class C campground**, a primitive camping area with 14 sites, is also available; it is closed during shotgun deer season. The **Youth Group camping area** is available on a first come, first served basis for organized groups with adult supervision. This area cannot be reserved in advance. For information, contact Giant City State Park, 235 Giant City Road, Makanda, IL, 62958, 618-457-4836.

- Hunting at Giant City is allowed on a controlled basis. Contact the site superintendent for season times and area rules at 618-457-4836. Proper registration rules are strictly enforced.

- Rock climbing/rappelling is permitted in two locations, the areas of Devil's Stand Table cliff and Shelter #1 bluff, at the Makanda entrance. Climbers must have their own equipment, and permanent anchors are not allowed. All climbing activities at the park are conducted at your own risk.

- Visit the rustic village of **Makanda,** just west of **Giant City State Park**. The tiny downtown offers a unique shopping experience and limited food and beverage items.

Giant City Lodge

Snowshoeing at Giant City State Park

Day Trip	Landforms and Features	Distance (round-trip) and Duration	Difficulty	Facilities
Giant City State Park Visitor center parking area 37°36′03.9″ N 89°11′19.1″ W	Massive sandstone bluffs and boulders, shelter caves	Giant City Nature Trail—1 mile, 1.5 hours	Moderate–difficult	Visitor center, lodge and cabins, picnic tables and shelters, water, fire grills, and children's playgrounds. Hunting, fishing, boating, horseback riding, rock climbing/rappelling. Class A and C campgrounds.
		Devil's Stand Table Trail—.25 mile, 30 minutes	Moderate–difficult	
		Indian Creek Nature Trail—1 mile, 45 minutes	Moderate	
		Post Oak Trail—.4 mile, 30 minutes	Easy	
		Stone Fort Trail—.5 mile, 30 minutes	Moderate	
		Trillium Trail—1.75 miles, 1 hour	Moderate–difficult	
		Red Cedar Trail (one must obtain a permit from the visitor center before using this trail)—16 miles	Difficult	

Directions

On IL-13 at the east edge of Carbondale, turn right (south) on Giant City Road and go 12 miles to the **Giant City State Park** entrance.

To heal mine aching moods,
give me God's virgin woods.
—Clinton Scollard

Day Trip 17

Hikers on the trail at Little Grand Canyon

To hike the entire loop of the **Little Grand Canyon** trail, start at the trailhead that leads north from the parking lot and look for the white diamonds on trees. There is really just one main trail at Little Grand Canyon, but do stay alert and aware of your surroundings. It is important not to wander off the trail, as people sometimes get lost in this area. The loop trail is scenic throughout with a wonderful diversity of natural features. You will be led into the canyon via steep sandstone creek beds, which have been made somewhat easier to negotiate by stone steps carved in the rocks by the Civilian Conservation Corps during

- Little Grand Canyon
- Pomona Natural Bridge

the 1930s. Wet sandstone is slippery, and caution is needed. The rock ledges are a natural habitat for snake dens, including such poisonous species as the copperhead, cottonmouth, and timber rattler. Once found in abundance here, the reptile population has declined over the years. It is illegal to take or kill any snake in the area. Be respectful of all the wildlife at Little Grand Canyon, which includes raccoons, minks, bobcats, deer, foxes, and birds.

Once you have descended the bluffs and reach the canyon floor, you will enter a different forest terrain, dominated by giant beech trees. Be prepared to step on rocks to cross streams as you continue through this lovely valley. Watch for scenic overlooks as the trail heads up out of the valley and along the ridge. From the Chalk Bluff overlook, you can see an open vista of the Mississippi River valley. Continue hiking upward along the ridge trail, and you will realize how high you have climbed when you find yourself at eye level with the tops of the trees lining the valley below. You may get the feeling that you are walking on air. The wildflowers in the spring and the fall colors are magnificent here. The last mile is through forest on either side of the trail. When we visited in October, the huge yellow pawpaw leaves were

Chalk Bluff overlook, Little Grand Canyon

Pomona Natural Bridge

bright and abundant, marking a gorgeous path through the woods. We highly recommend spending the time to hike the entire trail, but if time or physical conditions are limiting factors, you can start at the trailhead near the restrooms and head west toward the scenic overlooks. Once there, you can retrace your route to the parking lot and omit the descent into the canyon.

Finish your day by taking the short hike to see the remarkable **Pomona Natural Bridge.** Snug within a forest of mature oak, hickory, and beech trees, this arresting natural landmark has a quiet grandeur. You will catch your first glimpse of the bridge as you descend from the trail above the creek bottom where it is located. There is a small bluff area to explore, but the dominant feature here is the unexpectedly large natural bridge. Although the trail is short, the return trip is uphill, requiring an extra bit of effort. Both Little Grand Canyon and Pomona Natural Bridge are areas where you should take your time and enjoy a leisurely respite from the world of work. Breathe in the essence of the forest, and let nature work its soothing magic.

Just so you know . . .

- **Little Grand Canyon** is a deep box canyon with bluffs rising more than 300 feet above the Mississippi floodplain.

- There is no hunting, fishing, or camping at either Little Grand Canyon or **Pomona Natural Bridge**.

- Little Grand Canyon and Pomona Natural Bridge are both open year-round, but the recommended seasons to visit are spring, summer, and fall. Neither is wheelchair accessible.

- Flash floods can occur at Little Grand Canyon. Always be mindful of weather conditions.

- Pomona Natural Bridge spans 90 feet.

- For more information about Little Grand Canyon and Pomona Natural Bridge, contact Mississippi Bluffs Ranger District, 521 North Main, Jonesboro, IL, 62952, 618-833-8576.

Little Grand Canyon trail

Day Trip	Landforms and Features	Distance (round-trip) and Duration	Difficulty	Facilities
Little Grand Canyon 37°40′49.64″ N 89°23′41.49″ W	Deep box canyon, 300-foot sandstone bluffs, upper dryland forest, moist bottomland habitat	3.6-mile loop trail, 2.5–3 hours	Moderate– difficult	Parking, toilets, picnic tables, interpretive signs
Pomona Natural Bridge 37°38′55.12″ N 89°20′35.74″ W	90-foot sandstone bridge; oak, hickory, and beech forest	.5-mile loop trail, 30–45 minutes	Moderate	Parking, picnic tables

Directions

From Murphysboro to **Little Grand Canyon**, follow route IL-127 south for 5.8 miles to Etherton Road. Turn right (west) and continue 6.2 miles to Little Grand Canyon. Follow the posted signs along this good, all-weather road. Watch for the small sign directing you to the Little Grand Canyon parking area.

From Little Grand Canyon to **Pomona Natural Bridge**, retrace route to IL-127. Turn right (south) and go 4.2 miles to Pomona Road. Turn right (west) and go .7 mile to the small downtown Pomona area. Turn right (north) and continue 200 yards to Natural Bridge Road (gravel). Follow this road 2.2 miles to bridge parking. Keep right at the Y and follow posted signs. The road ends at the parking area.

Hikers at Little Grand Canyon

*I believe that there is a subtle magnetism
in Nature, which, if we unconsciously
yield to it, will direct us aright.*
—Henry David Thoreau

Day Trip 18

Pine Hills bluff

One of the big attractions drawing people to the **Pine Hills–
LaRue Swamp** area is the biannual "snake migration." We
have witnessed this event several times over the years, and it
is still fascinating to see, not just because of the abundance of
reptiles on view but also because of the people who turn out
to watch the snakes cross the road. The Forest Service closes a
2.5-mile segment of LaRue Road (Snake Road) each spring from
March 15 to May 15 and in the fall from September 1 to October 30 to allow the seasonal migration of the animals, which go
back and forth from the bluffs to the adjacent swamp, to proceed

- Pine Hills–
  LaRue Swamp

- Trail of Tears
  State Forest

Fire tower, Trail of Tears State Forest

without the hazard of vehicular traffic. People are still allowed to hike along the road during this time, and many do. From what we have observed, the reptiles seem intent upon migrating between their summer and winter habitats, and people watch this with respectful caution. Another favorite activity is to drive the bluff road, starting, for instance, at the north end near Snake Road and continuing through Pine Hills, stopping at various scenic overlooks or trailheads, and ending at the south end entrance near the campgrounds. Watch for the posted signs indicating various points of interest. Inspiration Point is one of the most popular trail destinations. If you enter Pine Hills from Muddy Levee Road, it is only a mile from the base of the bluff to the Inspiration Point parking area. Follow the directional signs and hike the trail up to the top of this high bluff, where you have a sweeping view of the Mississippi River valley. You may or may not want to continue to the rocky cliff edge for an even more panoramic view. This is not a place for people who are afraid of heights or have balance problems. Always exercise good judgment and extreme caution.

Complete your day at the **Trail of Tears State Forest**. This beautiful area was used extensively by prehistoric Native Americans and derives its name from its close proximity to the makeshift camps of Cherokee Indians who traveled this route, known as the "Trail of Tears," and endured the bitter winter of 1838–39. There are lovely picnic areas with rustic log and stone shelters, a legacy from the Civilian Conservation Corps that operated here during the 1930s, and many hiking trails, as well as the fire trails that are open all year for hiking. The varieties of forest trees vary, depending upon the terrain, which ranges from dry ridgetops to moist sites in stream valleys. In spring, the lower slopes and lush valleys support many native wildflowers, ferns, and flowering plants. Short and long trails are available, offering many opportunities to view songbirds and woodland mammals such as deer, foxes, squirrels, chipmunks, opossums, skunks, raccoons, and maybe even a coyote or bobcat. The two species of poisonous snakes that live here, the timber rattlesnake and the northern copperhead, are seldom seen, but always be cautious and respectful of this natural environment.

From December 24 to about the second week of May, gravel roads are closed to vehicles. When open, drive the graveled South Forest Road, a 2.6-mile, one-way loop through the heart of the forest that leads past the fire tower and several picturesque picnic and camping sites. These spots are off the beaten

LaRue Swamp vista

path from the paved road through the main public areas. You are certain to take pleasure in a visit to this Illinois state forest, one of the most beautiful and well-maintained recreational and protected areas that we have seen. This multiple-use site may be enjoyed at any time of year, but spring and fall are both outstanding times to visit.

Standing on Inspiration Point, Pine Hills

Cottonmouth snake at LaRue Swamp

Just so you know . . .

- **Pine Hills–LaRue Swamp/Otter Pond** is a permanently protected research natural area. Many of the 1,200 species of plants and animals living here are listed as threatened or endangered. Special restrictions apply to public use of this area. For more information, visit www.fs.fed.us/r9/forests/shawnee, call 618-253-7114, or write to Shawnee National Forest, Forest Supervisor's Office, Attn: RNA Coordinator, 50 Hwy. 145 S, Harrisburg, IL, 62946.

- The **Pine Hills Campground** includes 13 campsites and is open for use from March 15 to December 15. This is a primitive campground with privies. There is no electricity, drinking water, or showers.

- The closure of Snake Road at Pine Hills does not interfere with waterfowl hunting, a late fall activity in the LaRue Swamp.

- Both Class C and Class D camping sites are available at the **Trail of Tears State Forest** with some seasonal restrictions. For information, contact the site superintendent headquarters at 3240 State Forest Road, Jonesboro, IL, 62952, 618-833-4910.

- Horseback riding is permitted at the Trail of Tears State Forest along designated horse trails, with seasonal and trail condition restrictions. Call 618-833-4910 for information and to request a map of the horse trails.

- Hunting in designated areas at designated times is permitted at the Trail of Tears State Forest. All state and federal regulations apply.

- The **Union State Nursery**, occupying 120 acres of the Trail of Tears State Forest, is one of two Illinois plant propagation centers. The nursery produces up to 3 million seedlings a year.

- Pack a lunch. There are no concessions available at Pine Hills–LaRue Swamp or the Trail of Tears State Forest.

Day Trip	Landforms and Features	Distance (round-trip) and Duration	Difficulty	Facilities
Pine Hills– LaRue Swamp Snake Road (North) 37°35′5.83″ N 89°26′24.26″ W	350–400-foot limestone bluffs adjacent to swamp area	Snake Road—5 miles, 3–4 hours	Easy	Parking areas, privies, and picnic tables at various locations
Inspiration Point 37°35′7.07″ N 89°26′22.30″ W		.75 mile, 1 hour	Moderate– difficult	
Campground 37°30′56.97″ N 89°25′20.13″ W				13 sites, small fee, no electricity, no water
Trail of Tears State Forest Parking area near South Forest Rd. entrance 37°28′59.5″ N 89°21′33.7″ W	Dry, rocky ridgetops and narrow forested valleys; clear streams; under-story shrubs; wide diversity of flora, fauna, and mammal species	Short and long trails available, explore at will, 1–2 hours	Easy– moderate	Parking, interpre-tive signs, picnic areas with tables and drinking water, privies

Directions

From Murphysboro to **Pine Hills–LaRue Swamp**, take IL-149 west 7 miles to IL-3. Turn left (south) on IL-3 and drive 14 miles to Muddy Levee Road. Turn left (east) on Muddy Levee Road and proceed 2.8 miles to the base of Pine Hills Bluff. You will see a brown Forest Service sign directing you to locations within the Pine Hills ecological area.

From Pine Hills to the **Trail of Tears State Forest**, start at the bluff road (Forest Road 236) at the south end near the camp-grounds, turn left (east) on State Forest Road, and travel 4.1 miles to Fire Tower Road at the Trail of Tears State Forest. Turn right (south) on Fire Tower Road and follow this straight ahead to S. Forest Road. S. Forest Road is a one-way, narrow gravel road that makes a 2.6-mile loop through the forest. At .8 mile, you will see the fire tower. Follow directional signs along the paved road for visiting the main recreational areas within the park.

Between every two pines is
a doorway to a new world.
—John Muir

Day Trip 19

Tower Rock Island, Devil's Backbone Recreational Park

Piney Creek Ravine Nature Preserve is a rare place. You can walk up to a sandstone wall decorated with rock art believed to date to the Late Woodland (A.D. 500–1000) and Mississippian (A.D. 1000–1550) periods. Getting there is half the fun, and gazing on the evidence of prehistoric human habitation is a special kind of thrill. The hike starts out easily from the parking area as you walk through a meadow-like setting to a large sign directing you to the path that leads down into Piney Creek Ravine. The path becomes narrow and rutted, but there is good signage throughout the route, keeping you on the right track. You will cross a rocky streambed and continue to a crossroads in the trail. If you want to hike the loop trail that goes along the top of the bluff, you will turn in one direction, or you can follow the sign

- Piney Creek Ravine Nature Preserve

- Oakwood Bottoms

- Devil's Backbone Recreational Park

that points you to the rock art and go directly there. Take your time and follow the trail signs to see everything Piney Creek Ravine has to offer.

It is a disquieting thought to realize how easily this priceless area could be damaged. Please respect this gift of time and place by leaving no trace of yourself as you pass through. The rock art is not the only remarkable feature here; this is one of only two locations in Illinois where shortleaf pines grow naturally. There are also rare plant species to identify and bird-watching opportunities year-round.

From Piney Creek Ravine, continue to **Oakwood Bottoms**, a place where Shawnee Forest managers have teamed with such agencies as Ducks Unlimited, Inc., the National Wild Turkey Federation, the National Fish and Wildlife Foundation, the National Forest Foundation, and the Illinois Department of Natural Resources to provide a migratory waterfowl and wetland wildlife habitat while embracing the total ecosystem of bottomland hardwoods. Greentree reservoirs, forested sites that are flooded during the winter months and drained for the growing season, were created to provide habitats for waterfowl in the fall and winter months. This prolonged flooding, while good for the waterfowl, was not good for the pin oaks that had been planted to help reestablish the native forest. Oakwood Bottoms is still a work in progress, but a new flooding regime combined with vegetation and water management will help ensure the health of the pin oak forest. Visitors may walk the nature trail or quietly view wildlife from a wheelchair accessible blind. There are two warm-water ponds for fishing, and hunting of squirrels, ducks, turkeys, and deer is allowed in season.

One last stop will complete your day with a visit to **Devil's Backbone Recreational Park** in Grand Tower. This park/campground is right along the Mississippi River beachfront and has lovely views of the river and the famous Tower Rock landmark. Walk along the shoreline and gaze across the river to the state of Missouri. It is hard to imagine from the Illinois side, but it has been said that during periods of dry weather, it is possible to walk out to Tower Rock Island from the Missouri shoreline. The beauty of the river can be enjoyed at any time of the year. Each season has its own compelling aspects as the water maintains its endless flow.

Just so you know . . .

- **Piney Creek Ravine Nature Preserve** consists of 198 acres purchased in 1972 for its natural features and rare plant specimens.

- Piney Creek rock art includes prehistoric pictographs (paintings) and petroglyphs (designs pecked into the soft sandstone by using a small hard rock as a hammer).

- To report any disturbance or vandalism to the rock art at Piney Creek Ravine, contact the site superintendent at the Randolph State Fish and Wildlife Area, 4301 S. Lake Drive, Chester, IL, 62233, 618-826-2706.

- In the 1800s, there were 25 million acres of bottomland hardwood forest from Southern Illinois to the Gulf of Mexico. **Oakwood Bottoms** represents a managed attempt to mimic a natural, thriving bottomland hardwood forest filled with plants and animals.

- **Devil's Backbone Campground** facilities include water, electricity, dump station, restrooms, and showers on site. For information, call 618-684-6192. (This is not a Shawnee National Forest campground.)

Piney Creek petroglyph bluff

Greentree Reservoir at Oakwood Bottoms

Piney Creek Trail

Day Trip	Landforms and Features	Distance (round-trip) and Duration	Difficulty	Facilities
Piney Creek Ravine Nature Preserve 37°53′56″ N 89°38′14″ W	80-foot-deep canyon, sandstone bluffs, rocky streams, upland forest dominated by post and blackjack oaks, moist ravine forest including beech and tulip poplar, ancient petroglyphs and pictographs	2.5-mile loop trail, 3 hours	Easy-moderate	Parking area, interpretive signs
Oakwood Bottoms Greentree reservoir parking area 37°40′28.4″ N 89°27′43.7″ W	3,600 acres of managed wetlands and bottomland hardwood forest	Hiking trail around reservoir (.25-mile loop, 25 minutes), wildlife viewing blind (100 yards), drive through campground area, 1.5 hours total	Easy	Parking, accessible viewing platform at wetlands observation site, interpretive signs, picnic shelter and trash receptacle at greentree reservoir, picnic tables, fire rings, vehicle access at Turkey Bayou Campground
Devil's Backbone Recreational Park Campground 37°38′16″ N 89°30′40″ W Public boat launch area 37°37′49.8″ N 89°30′21.9″ W	Mississippi River, Tower Rock Island	Walk the shoreline, 1 hour	Easy	Parking, picnic tables, campground, food at convenience store in Grand Tower

Directions

From Murphysboro to **Piney Creek Ravine Nature Preserve**, go west on IL-149 for 8 miles to the IL-3 junction. Turn right (north) on IL-3, continuing 11 miles to Hog Hill Road. Turn right (north) on Hog Hill Road and continue for 4 miles to a T. Turn right (east) for just a very short distance to Rock Crusher Road. Turn left (north) on Rock Crusher Road and continue for 1.2 miles. At the next T, turn left (west), continuing for 1.5 miles to a parking lot on the right side of the road. There is a large sign in the parking area, but it is hard to see until you are almost past it. The parking area is off a small curve in the road.

From the Piney Creek parking area to **Oakwood Bottoms**, retrace route to IL-3. Turn left (east) on IL-3 and go 17.7 miles to Oakwood Bottoms Road. Turn left (east) onto this gravel road and travel .7 mile to the wetlands observation platform. From here to the greentree reservoir area, continue traveling east on Oakwood Bottoms Road (Forest Road 786) for .1 mile. Turn left (north), as a greentree reservoir sign indicates, and continue the short distance to the parking area. To reach Turkey Bayou Campground, return to Oakwood Bottoms Road and continue traveling east for 2.8 miles to where the road comes to a dead end at the Big Muddy Boat Launch parking area. Follow an offshoot road to the north, as a sign indicates, for .5 mile to the Turkey Bayou Campground, where the road comes to a dead end.

From Oakwood Bottoms to **Devil's Backbone Recreational Park**, retrace route to IL-3. Turn left (south) on IL-3 and go 3.3 miles to Grand Tower Road. Turn right (west), continuing for 1 mile to the village of Grand Tower. Turn right (north) on 3rd Street, which heads downtown. Take the levee road on your left and go 75 yards. This is a great vantage point to view and photograph Tower Rock Island, located in the Mississippi River. Continue north on the levee road (about .5 mile) and turn left to the entrance of Devil's Backbone Campground. Make an immediate right (north) on the gravel road that dead-ends (250 yards) at the Mississippi River.

Adopt the pace of nature: her secret is patience.
—Ralph Waldo Emerson

Day Trip 20

Lower trail of Wildcat Bluff

How about a long hike through an upland forest, across the Cache River, past a hand-hewed log cabin, and into an area containing one of the finest remaining cypress swamps in the state? From the **Wildcat Bluff** parking area, a narrow path leads to an open area containing a large Forest Service sign and brochures. From here, you may choose the trailhead to your left (east) that follows the top of the bluff for about half a mile to a lookout point and back, or you may choose the much longer trailhead to your right (west) that leads to Boss Island and **Little Black Slough**.

If you decide to tackle the longer trail, you have another choice to make. Do you want to remain on top of the bluff and walk the

- Wildcat Bluff
- Little Black Slough

Cache River crossing to Boss Island

relatively smooth road to begin, or do you want to descend to the base of the bluff and follow the lower path for the first 250 yards or so, past very scenic sandstone ridges, until you ascend and rejoin the upper trail? The path down to the base of the bluff, accessed near the lookout point trailhead, requires scrambling straight down a narrow rocky crevice and following a rough and rutted but obvious trail. If you have the necessary agility, the views of the sandstone bluff and overhangs are worth the effort.

The upper trail, Little Black Slough Trail, is really an old road leading to an area that has come to be called Boss Island. John and Christiana Bost were the first settlers to build a cabin in this area, surrounded by Little Black Slough and the Cache River. They built their two-room home in the fall of 1853 and proceeded to raise a family that eventually included eight children. Boss Island derives its name from the original Bost family, but when the name change occurred is unknown. It takes about 40 minutes of steady hiking to reach the Bost cabin from the Wildcat Bluff trailhead. The road meanders through the predominately oak and hickory forest relatively smoothly. At 1.5 miles from the trailhead, you will cross a rocky ford on the Cache River, which is difficult during high water, to access Boss Island. From here it is a short distance to the Bost cabin, standing alone in a small open glade. This is the only structure left of a tiny community known as Scanlin Spur. The Bost cabin was inhabited as late as 1955 but never had electricity or running water. Continue past the cabin and cross the railroad tracks. The trail comes to a Y intersection, with Forest Service signs indicating trail destinations.

Little Black Slough Trail makes a loop through a bottomland forest with oak, hickory, sweet gum, and catalpa trees. If you start off to the left from the Y intersection, you will come to a view of the cypress swamp area, known as Little Black Slough, after about half a mile. The trail parallels the swamp for a while and then gradually turns away from the swamp and through the forest trees, eventually arriving back at the Y intersection. From the Y, you will retrace your route all the way to the parking lot. Since this is an old road, the trail is wider than most foot paths and allows easier walking. It is also an unmistakable path through the woods, so there is little danger of losing your way. In the winter, when the leaves are gone from the trees, there is a more open view of Little Black Slough and no insects to combat, making this a good choice for a cold-weather hike. Whenever you visit, make this a leisurely stroll and pause at the Bost cabin to consider what it must have been like growing up here in the middle to late 1800s.

The best view of Little Black Slough, though, is achieved by approaching it from the Marshall Ridge Access point. Instead of making the complete 5.5-mile hike at Wildcat Bluff, you could hike the trail as far as the Bost cabin and then return to the parking lot. Then, drive over to the Marshall Ridge Access point at the Cache River State Natural Area Office at Belknap. The trail to Little Black Slough is about a mile and a half shorter than the trail at Wildcat Bluff and offers a more continuous view of the swamp.

Just so you know . . .

- **Wildcat Bluff** and **Little Black Slough** are within the Cache River State Natural Area that contains more than 21 miles of designated foot trails.

- Canoeists can enjoy a three- to six-mile canoe trail through the Lower Cache River cypress/tupelo swamp. The launching point is the **Lower Cache River Access** area south of Perks. Canoe maps and fact sheets are available at the site headquarters, 930 Sunflower Lane, Belknap, IL, 62908, 618-634-9678.

- Carry food and water with you for this hike. There are no concessions available in this area.

Little Black Slough

Day Trip	Landforms and Features	Distance (round-trip) and Duration	Difficulty	Facilities
Wildcat Bluff Parking area 37°22′35.1″ N 88°55′43.4″ W	Sandstone bluff with vistas of the Cache River bottomlands	Lookout Point Trail—1 mile, 30 minutes	Easy	Parking area, sign and brochures
		Lower Bluff Trail— 250 yards	Difficult	
		Little Black Slough Trail—5.5 miles, 3–4 hours	Moderate	
Little Black Slough (Marshall Ridge Access) Cache River State Natural Area Office at Belknap 37°20′06.1″ N 88°56′17.7″ W	Bald cypress and tupelo swamps accessed by a trail past sandstone bluffs and floodplain forests	Little Black Slough/ Tupelo Trail—4 miles, 2 hours	Moderate	Parking area, signs, wheelchair accessible restroom, Michael W. Wolff Memorial Wetlands viewing platform

Bost cabin, Wildcat Bluff Trail

Cache River at Wildcat Bluff

Directions

From the junction of IL-45 and IL-146 at Vienna, travel south on IL-45 for 2.9 miles to the **Wildcat Bluff** sign (Ballowe Church Road). Turn right (west) as indicated by the sign and drive 3.4 miles to Wildcat Bluff Road. (Watch for a small Wildcat Bluff sign at 1.8 miles just prior to a bridge. Go left [west] at this fork and then 1.6 miles to Wildcat Bluff Road.) Turn left (south) onto Wildcat Bluff Road and continue for .7 mile to the parking area on the left-hand side of a dead-end road. The route is marked, but the signs are small and easy to miss. Watch carefully. **Little Black Slough** is reached on foot from the Wildcat Bluff trailhead.

To reach the **Marshall Ridge Access** from Wildcat Bluff, retrace route to IL-45 at Ballowe Church Road entrance. Turn right (south) on IL-45 and go 2.1 miles to Belknap Road. Turn right (west) on Belknap Road and continue 4.1 miles to Belknap. Turn right (west) on W. Main Street and go .2 mile to Sunflower Lane. Turn right (north) on Sunflower Lane and go 1.1 miles to the Cache River State Natural Area Office parking lot. A sign at the west edge of the parking area indicates a gravel road leading to Marshall Ridge Access. Follow this road (north) for .6 mile to the **Michael W. Wolff Memorial Wetlands**. There is a large parking area at the end of this road and a wheelchair accessible restroom. Signs indicate hiking trails to Little Black Slough or Heron Pond. There is a wheelchair accessible area, close to the parking lot, for viewing the Michael W. Wolff Memorial Wetlands. A large interpretive sign details information about the wetlands.

Special Attractions

Special Attractions

John O'Dell, founder and chairman of the River-to-River Trail Society

Southern Illinois tourism has received a major boost in recent years from the development of two very special attractions, the River-to-River Trail and the Shawnee Hills American Viticultural Area (AVA). While they have had a similarly positive impact of bringing people to Southern Illinois, the two experiences could not be more different.

The **River-to-River Trail**, when hiked in its entirety, is a daunting 160 miles or so of unsurpassed wilderness beauty. This is not a journey to be undertaken lightly. Hikers wishing to complete the entire trail generally travel from east to west, starting at the Ohio River near the Rose Hotel in Elizabethtown and ending at Devil's Backbone Recreational Park near Grand Tower on

- River-to-River Trail
- Shawnee Hills American Viticultural Area

the Mississippi River. A common ritual is for the long-distance hiker to collect a small amount of water from the Ohio River and release it into the Mississippi River upon completion of the trip. Long-distance hiking is totally different from day trip hiking. The long-distance hiker has opportunities to encounter wildlife and view some truly amazing scenery not available to the casual day hiker, who is able to return to a comfortable bed and hot food at the end of the day. It takes most hikers two to three weeks to travel the entire river-to-river distance. Careful planning and forethought are essential.

An indispensable aid is the *River-to-River Trail Guide*, available from the River-to-River Trail Society, a not-for-profit corporation founded in 1990 for the trail's preservation and upkeep. This wonderful resource, now in its fourth edition, provides detailed maps, GPS locations, and trail descriptions combined with some interesting history and local folklore; proceeds from this publication provide the funding for signage and other expenses of the society. According to John O'Dell, founder and current chairman of the River-to-River Trail Society, the most common error made by long-distance hikers is underestimating the wilderness aspect of the trail and overestimating the amount of weight they can carry in their backpacks. Of course, the River-to-River Trail can be enjoyed in smaller segments. O'Dell estimates that only about half of the people who use the trail are "through" hikers. No particular statistics are kept concerning trail usage, in keeping with the general philosophy that this is an independent and private journey. Day hikers, equestrians, and backpackers all use the trail and benefit from its existence. It takes many hours of labor from volunteer workers to keep the trail maintained each year. Southern Illinois is fortunate to have this dedicated group of people working to keep our beautiful and unique wilderness areas available for the public to enjoy.

Southern Illinois offers more than a wilderness experience for travelers, though. Since its inception in the mid-1990s, the Shawnee Hills Wine Trail has offered visitors the pleasant experience of sampling locally produced wines along an established route of independent Southern Illinois vineyards. The **Shawnee Hills** is a federally recognized **American Viticultural Area**, meaning that this area of Southern Illinois is a designated wine-grape-growing region in the United States with distinct geographic features. The Shawnee Hills Wine Trail Association (south of Route 13 and west of Interstate 57) is the largest organization of wineries within the southwestern portion of the AVA. The Southern Illinois Wine Trail also includes locations east of Interstate 57. Most of the Shawnee National Forest is included in the Shawnee Hills AVA geographical region.

The development of these wineries has provided a great boost to the local economy, fostering growth in lodging for tourists (such as bed-and-breakfast establishments and vacation cabin rentals), generating revenue from product sales, and creating employment opportunities. The wineries vary in size and the elaborateness of entertainment offerings. Some of the larger establishments host live musical entertainment on a regular basis and sponsor large festivals at various times of the year. According to Jim Ewers, current president of the Shawnee Hills Wine Trail Association, there is a great variety of offerings produced by the various vintners, and the regional brand is slowly gaining prestige as each vineyard works toward developing high-quality, world-class wines. The stunning beauty of the Shawnee National Forest is surely a major component in the successful growth of this tourist industry. Pairing a quality local product with the majestic beauty of the geographical environment is an unbeatable recipe for success.

A winery on the Shawnee Hills Wine Trail

For More Information

River-to-River Trail	Shawnee National Forest Supervisor's Office 50 Hwy. 145 S Harrisburg, IL 62946 618-253-7114 River-to-River Trail Society 1142 Winkleman Rd. Harrisburg, IL 62946 618-252-6789 www.rivertorivertrail.com
Shawnee Hills Wine Trail Association	Southernmost Tourism Bureau P.O. Box 378 Anna, IL 62906 1-800-248-4373 www.shawneehillswinetrail.com
Southern Illinois Wine Trail	Williamson County Tourism Bureau 1602 Sioux Dr. Marion, IL 62959 618-997-3690 or 800-433-7399 www.visitsi.com/wineries

Illinois Department of Natural Resources

Emergency Information

Index

Illinois Department of Natural Resources

Region V Park Offices

Cache River State Natural Area, 930 Sunflower Lane, Belknap,
   IL, 62908, 618-634-9678.
South Region District Office, 1812 Grinnell Road, Belknap, IL,
   62908, 618-524-5577.

Shawnee National Forest Contact Information

Hidden Springs Ranger District, 602 N. First Street, Route 45
   North, Vienna, IL, 62995. Front desk, 618-658-2111 or 618-
   287-2201. Office hours, Monday–Friday, 8:00 A.M.–4:30 P.M.
Mississippi Bluffs Ranger District, 521 North Main, Jonesboro,
   IL, 62952, 618-833-8576 or 618-687-1731, www.fs.fed.us/r9/
   forests/shawnee, http://fs.usda.gov/shawnee.
Shawnee National Forest Supervisor's Office, 50 Hwy. 145 South,
   Harrisburg, IL, 62946. Information desk, 618-253-7114.

Internet Website

www.dnr.illinois.gov. Follow links for information to specific locations within the Shawnee National Forest, including camp-
   ing/fishing/hunting sites and regulations, license permits,
   and fees.

Disclaimer

Actions by nature can result in closed roads/trails and other
facilities. Call ahead to the park office before you make your trip.

Remember
Take only memories, leave only footprints

Emergency Information

Weather

Paducah: 270-744-6440
St. Louis: 636-441-8467

Hospitals

Harrisburg Medical Center: 618-253-7671
Heartland Regional Medical Center (Marion): 618-998-7000
Lourdes (Paducah): 270-444-2444
Massac Memorial (Metropolis): 618-524-2176
Memorial Hospital of Carbondale: 618-549-0721
Saint Francis Medical Center (Cape Girardeau): 573-331-3000
Southeast (Cape Girardeau): 573-334-4822
St. Joseph Memorial (Murphysboro): 618-684-3156
Union County (Anna): 618-833-4511
Western Baptist (Paducah): 270-575-2100

State Police

Carmi: 618-382-1911
Du Quoin: 618-542-2171
Ullin: 618-845-3740

Local Sheriffs' Offices

Alexander County: 618-734-2141
Jackson County: 618-684-2177 or 618-687-3822
Johnson County: 618-658-8264
Massac County: 618-524-2912
Pulaski County: 618-748-9374
Randolph County: 618-826-5484
Saline County: 618-252-8661
Union County: 618-833-5500
Williamson County: 618-998-2150

Index

Page numbers in boldface italics indicate illustrations.

Larry P. Mahan holds a bachelor's degree in education from Western Illinois University and a master's degree in administration from Sangamon State University (now the University of Illinois, Springfield). In 1975, Larry received the Educational Excellence, Regional Outstanding Teacher Award from the Illinois Office of Education. In addition to his classroom experience, Larry has served as both an elementary and a high school principal in a career spanning 50 years in the field of education. Now retired, Larry has found and registered over 30 Illinois Big Tree Champions and has chronicled this experience in his book *In Search of Large Trees*. He holds the office of South Palmyra Township clerk and is a member of the Oak Hill Cemetery board.

Donna J. Mahan holds a bachelor's degree in music from Southern Illinois University Carbondale. Her career in education spans 27 years and includes classroom music teaching at the kindergarten through high school levels, as well as vocal and instrumental instruction. Now retired, Donna is the music director of the Northwestern Area Community Choir.

Jointly authored articles by Larry and Donna have been published in *Springhouse* magazine. Since the early 1990s, the Mahans have been planting trees on their 20-acre farm, the Mahan Arboretum, which includes more than 100 different species. Most of the trees are native to Illinois, and several were grown from collected seed, including some from county, state, and national champions. The Mahan Arboretum was a featured location on the Macoupin County Master Gardeners 2011 tour.

 *A Shawnee Book*

Also available in this series . . .